Inflation and Unemployment

To Mair

Author's note
Following common convention the term billion indicates thousand million.

Printed and bound in Great Britain by
Billing and Sons Ltd, Worcester

Inflation and Unemployment

Causes, Consequences and Cures

Graham Dawson
Lecturer in Economics
The Open University

Edward Elgar

Published by
Edward Elgar Publishing Limited
Gower House
Croft Road
Aldershot
Hants GU11 3HR
England

Edward Elgar Publishing Company
Old Post Road
Brookfield
Vermont 05036
USA

A CIP catalogue record for this book is available from the British Library

Library of Congress Cataloging-in-Publication Data
Dawson, Graham.
    Inflation and unemployment: causes, consequences and cures/ Graham Dawson.   p.   cm.
    Includes bibliographical references and index.
    1. Unemployment – Great Britain – Costs. 2. Unemployment – United States – Costs. 3. Inflation (Economics) – Great Britain. 4. Inflation (Economics) – United States. 5. Unemployment – Great Britain – Effect of inflation on. 6. Unemployment – United States – Effect of inflation on. I. Title.

ISBN 1 85278 119 X
       1 85278 658 2 (paperback)

Contents

Tables

Figures

Acknowledgements

The acknowledgements written by a number of American authors of recent economics books have achieved a level of effusiveness and biographical detail that I, with my English reticence, would find it embarrassing to emulate. These words are no less sincere for being limited in number and restrained in tone.

This book has grown out of a pamphlet which Mark Blaug commissioned from me when we were working for the Employment Research Centre at the University of Buckingham. In pointing me in the direction of the question of whether the costs of unemployment are greater or less than the costs of inflation, Mark set me on a journey through such interesting and under-explored terrain that I am delighted to realize that the destination, in the shape of an established consensus, will remain over the horizon for a long time to come. He has remained an indefatigable source of sound advice and a mentor at once relentless in the detection of error and generous in the offering of encouragement.

I am grateful to my wife Mair for pouring scorn on my more pompous pronouncements and identifying at least one intellectual cul-de-sac before I wasted too much time searching for the main road to which I thought it was leading. She has also made certain that I have not neglected to acknowledge my third debt of gratitude, to the Thatcher government. To replicate at the end of the 1980s the monetarist experiment conducted at their beginning, presumably to allay any nagging doubts about the decisiveness of the result the first time around, is surely to carry scientific rigour to unwarranted extremes. My consternation as the events of the last few years ran their inevitable course has certainly given the book a polemical edge and a sense of urgency it might otherwise have lacked.

PART I
The Measurement and Explanation of Unemployment and Inflation

1. The Greater Evil: Unemployment or Inflation?

1.1 TWO QUESTIONS ABOUT THE COSTS OF UNEMPLOYMENT AND INFLATION

The main purpose of this book is the polemical one of answering the question: Are the governments of the advanced industrial nations right to have turned their backs on full employment as a policy objective and to be aiming instead at stable prices? It is polemical in that the question belongs to political debate rather than the pursuit of knowledge for its own sake. But the political issue inevitably raises another, more academic question: What do we know about the adverse effects of unemployment and inflation and the relationship between these two phenomena? This question leads naturally to a discussion of the difficulties encountered in trying to find out how unemployment and inflation might be related and what their respective costs might be. The principal focus of this discussion is on the arguments put forward by right-of-centre economists such as Milton Friedman, Friedrich von Hayek and Patrick Minford. However, the book is the result of a sufficiently wide trawl through the oceans of recent research to comprise a summary if not an encyclopaedia of the present state of knowledge on inflation and unemployment. And what *do* we know about these perennial problems of macroeconomics? We know enough to be confident that unemployment does much more damage to the economy and to people's lives than inflation. So my answer to the polemical question is, No – there is no basis in economic analysis for the conservative or new right belief that inflation is the root of all economic evil.

According to Professor Wynne Godley, that belief has become the current macroeconomic orthodoxy:

Another thing that deeply concerns me about the whole public discussion of economic policy at the moment is that the great tradi-

3

tional goals of economic policy, with the important exception of price stability, are disappearing from view. In particular, growth and unemployment are ceasing to be seen as objectives of policy, but rather as natural events . . . which the government can neither predict nor control. (Professor Wynne Godley, *New Statesman*, 15 March 1991)

Certainly, a central feature of the conservative revolution in macroeconomic policy which characterized the early 1980s was the abandonment of the assumption that policy makers had to juggle a set of partly conflicting objectives. The trick was to keep the stable prices plate in the air without letting growth and full employment fall to the ground. Policy was the art of the trade-off: how much inflation could be tolerated to sustain high growth and keep unemployment down until the next election; how much unemployment would be forgiven and forgotten by the time the election after that one came around. The macroeconomic world became much simpler in 1979; it flattened to the one-dimensional policy stance of eliminating inflation. If Professor Godley is right, the revolutionary cry of the 1970s became the conventional wisdom of the 1980s.

The polemical aim of this book is to challenge that orthodoxy. Is it really so important to defeat inflation that it is worth sacrificing millions of jobs in the battle? Can it really be true that if left unrestrained the tiger of inflation will inevitably cause even greater havoc? Having reviewed the evidence, my answer to both questions is no. Policy makers in the UK and the US overstated the dangers of inflation and understated both the amount of unemployment needed to curb it and the damage it would do. The positive thesis advanced here urges a return to the earlier orthodoxy, to the idea that policy makers continually juggle inflation and unemployment in search of the combination that minimizes the misery they both cause.

Both economic theories and political attitudes concerning inflation and unemployment have taken shape in response to two cataclysmic episodes which dominated the economic history of the first half of the twentieth century: the German hyperinflation of 1922–23 and mass unemployment throughout the industrialized world in the 1930s.

1.2   THE GERMAN HYPERINFLATION

The main point is that the objective of the authorities, pursued with
such means as are at their command, should be the stability of prices.
(Keynes, 1931, p. 92)

Those words were written within ten years of the German hyperinflation which had caused the collapse of commercial activity and
plunged the country into social and political chaos. The simplest
way to envisage the scale of the inflation is to remember that
inflation means the loss of a currency's purchasing power. What
you could have bought for 1 mark in July 1921 would have cost
54 000 million marks in November 1923. In two years inflation had
wiped out many people's savings, transforming a fortune into
useless small change. Imagine leaving £54 000 million cash in the
bank today while you spend two years sailing around the world or
working in Africa for Save the Children, only to find on your
return that your cash will buy you – four Mars bars.

It is therefore no surprise that, putting it as drily as possible, the
marginal propensity to consume equals one during hyperinflation.
People spend all their income as soon as possible after they receive
it in an effort to beat the next leap in prices. In Germany in 1922
many shopkeepers closed only a few hours after opening in order
to spend their takings before they became worthless – a self-
defeating strategy if adopted universally. Waves of panic buying
left shops with nothing left to sell, while manufacturers, operating
at full capacity, refused to accept new orders. In the final stages
of the hyperinflation foreign currencies and emergency monies
issued by state governments, chambers of commerce and private
traders replaced the mark until 2 000 different currencies were
thought to be in circulation. Eventually the absence of a single
widely acceptable means of exchange brought commerce to a halt,
closed factories, threw thousands of people out of work and even
threatened the inhabitants of some towns with starvation.

The events of 1923 in Germany instilled so deep a fear of
inflation into the hearts of British politicians that they eschewed
expansionary monetary and fiscal policies when faced with mass
unemployment in the 1930s.

1.3   MASS UNEMPLOYMENT IN THE 1930s

Among those who lost most in the German hyperinflation were those who had most to lose: the middle classes who owned financial assets denominated in money terms. Mass unemployment, however, inflicted hardship mainly on the poorest sections of society, the households of men who had been out of work for six months or more, who were married with several children and who when employed held only low-paid jobs.

> I have six little children to take care of. I have been out of work for over a year and a half. Am back almost thirteen months and the landlord says if I don't pay up before the 1 of 1932 out I must go, and where am I to go in the cold winter with my children? If you can help me please for God's sake and the children's sakes and like please do what you can and send me some help, will you, I cannot find any work. I am willing to take any kind of work if I could get it now. Thanksgiving dinner was black coffee and bread and was very glad to get it. My wife is in the hospital now. We have no shoes to were [*sic*]; no clothes hardly. Oh what will I do I sure will thank you. (Meltzer, 1969, p. 103)

Being unemployed had a lot to do with the misfortune of being in the wrong place at the wrong time. In the UK in 1932, for example, unemployment rates varied from 13.5 per cent in London to 36.5 per cent in Wales. The injustice was made worse by the absence of uniform and comprehensive social security benefits. Wide regional variations in benefit entitlements were revealed in 1933 by an official survey which asked 80 county boroughs to assess nine specimen cases. 'The results were predictably haphazard, ranging from £12 11s (£12.55) apportioned by West Ham to £3 12s 6d (£3.63) from Blackpool . . .' (Whiteside, 1987, p. 20).

The memory of mass unemployment led politicians throughout the industrialized world to make full employment a principal objective of macroeconomic policy in the postwar period.

1.4   FROM POSTWAR ORTHODOXY TO CONSERVATIVE REVOLUTION

Until the mid-1970s macroeconomic policy was based on the premiss that it was the government's duty to run the economy as close to full employment as possible, and guided by a supplementary assumption that the instruments of demand management had brought it within the government's competence to make 'as close to full employment as possible' very close indeed for most of the time. The constraint was that the risk of inflation was greatest near full employment, so every so often fiscal or monetary policy would be tightened to damp down the inflationary embers at the cost of a small and temporary increase in unemployment. Once the threat of inflation had receded, the economy could be reflated back towards full employment until the next upswing in prices.

The postwar orthodoxy presupposed that inflation and unemployment were inversely related; a little less unemployment could always be had at the cost of a little more inflation, and vice versa. But in the 1970s this trade-off appeared to break down. In the UK the Labour government responded by acknowledging the limits of demand management, in effect admitting that full employment was no longer a feasible objective:

> We used to think that you could just spend your way out of recession, and increase employment, by cutting taxes and boosting government spending. I tell you in all candour that that option no longer exists, and that in so far as it ever did exist, it worked by injecting inflation into the economy. (Mr James Callaghan, Labour Party Conference, September 1976)

This idea was taken further by the Conservative government, which believed that over the long term higher inflation was not only invariably followed by but actually caused higher unemployment:

> Some people think we can choose between inflation and unemployment. Let inflation rise a bit they say to get unemployment down. But it doesn't work like that. The two go together. Higher inflation means higher unemployment. It's like an addictive drug, the more you get the more you need and the more damage it does to you. (Mr Geoffrey Howe, Budget broadcast, 10 March 1981)

If inflation causes unemployment, the answer to the question of which is the greater evil is obvious, for the adverse effects or costs of unemployment are nothing other than the indirect or second-round costs of inflation. A causes B and B causes C, so A indirectly causes C. And the way to get rid of C is evidently to get rid of A.

1.5   TWO ARGUMENTS FOR DISINFLATION

There are therefore two distinct lines of argument for the conservative belief 'that the elimination of inflation should take precedence over all other economic objectives' (Sir Douglas Wass, Permanent Secretary to the Treasury 1974–83, *The Times*, 31 March 1983). The first version of the case for disinflation could be made from within the postwar orthodoxy. The two premisses of the argument are (i) that the costs of inflation are greater than the costs of unemployment and (ii) that inflation and unemployment are negatively correlated, from which the conclusion follows that it is better to tolerate higher unemployment in order to get rid of inflation than to put up with higher inflation in order to reduce unemployment. The second version of the case for disinflation rests on the rejection of the inflation/unemployment trade-off and hence of the postwar orthodoxy. The point here is simply that inflation causes unemployment. If that is true, even those whose ultimate objective is to achieve full employment have to agree that the elimination of inflation is an indispensable intermediate objective.

The dual nature of the controversy determines the structure of this book. In Part II the costs of unemployment and the costs of inflation are considered separately, in abstraction from the question of how inflation and unemployment are related. This approach really belongs to the postwar orthodoxy, in that the aim is to establish the truth or falsity of premiss (i) in the first version of the case for disinflation. So Chapters 7, 8 and 9 examine the costs of unemployment, while Chapters 10 and 11 investigate the costs of inflation. It will be argued that the costs of unemployment far outweigh those of inflation at the rates experienced by the UK and the US since 1970.

It is in Part III that the question of the relation between unemployment and inflation is discussed. The question is whether premiss (ii) of the first version of the case for disinflation is true or whether, as the second version holds, inflation causes unemployment. So Chapters 12 and 13 trace the development of the theory of the natural rate of unemployment. It will be argued that this is not after all an insurmountable obstacle in the way of the inflation/unemployment trade-off of the postwar orthodoxy. The implication is that disinflation is not painless, that reducing let alone eliminating inflation does involve costs in terms of lower growth and higher unemployment. In Chapters 14 and 15 conflicting interpretations of rational expectations theory are explored in an effort to quantify the costs of disinflation under different policy and institutional circumstances. The case for repudiating the new right claim that inflation must be eliminated 'whatever the short term consequences' is summed up in Chapter 16.

But there are important preliminary issues to be clarified before the costs of unemployment and inflation can be investigated and the relation between inflation and unemployment examined. Part I will attempt to elucidate the problems of defining, measuring and explaining unemployment and inflation.

2. Defining and Measuring Inflation

2.1 DEFINING INFLATION

Inflation is a sustained rise in the general level of prices or a persistent fall in the value of money. An overnight once-for-all rise in the prices of all the goods bought and sold in the economy does not in itself constitute inflation. The inflationary process only gets under way as one general price rise follows another. A sustained rise in the price of a single commodity is not in itself inflationary because it might be cancelled out by a sustained fall in the price of another. The inflationary process only gets under way when there is a sustained rise in the average level of prices. This general and persistent rise in the level of prices is the same thing as a continuing fall in the value of money. Money has value in so far as it can be used to buy goods and services. If those goods and services rise in price, the amount that can be bought with a given sum of money, its purchasing power, falls. Hence the two ways of defining inflation: it is a persistent rise in the general level of prices or (which is the same thing) a sustained fall in the value of money.

The implication of this double-sided definition is that any rate of inflation will eventually reduce the value of a fixed sum of money so much that it becomes useless. When this happens quickly it is known as hyperinflation. Government policy to reduce a moderate rate of inflation may ultimately be grounded in the fear that if unchecked an apparently harmless 3 per cent annual inflation rate inevitably turns into 30, 300 and even 3 000 per cent.

2.2 MEASURING INFLATION

The value of money changes whenever there is a rise or fall in the prices of the goods and services it is used to buy. There is no single and uncontroversially correct way of measuring the rate at which prices are rising. The basic reason is that the prices of the goods I buy might be rising more or less quickly than the prices of the goods you buy. There is no answer to the question 'Whose inflation rate is *the* inflation rate?'. All that can be done is to average the two. The rate of change of the prices of the goods and services bought by the average household is measured by the general index of retail prices (RPI) in the UK and by the consumer price index (CPI) in the US. Each month field workers make price observations by personal visits or telephone calls to shops. The RPI and the CPI are not simple averages of all the price changes observed, because some of the things people buy are more important than others in terms of the amount of money spent on them. For example, a 2 per cent rise in the price of bread has about four times the effect on the RPI as a 2 per cent rise in the price of butter. The RPI and the CPI allow for this by weighting each price change according to the amount of money spent on it by the average household.

The rate of inflation is calculated by multiplying each price change by its weighting and dividing the sum of these weighted price changes by the sum of the weights. Table 2.1 shows a hypothetical price index similar in basic principle to the RPI and the CPI. Twenty-one per cent of the average household's budget is spent on food, so a 10 per cent increase in the price of food results in a weighted price rise of 210. This is added to the other weighted price rises and the total is divided by the sum of the weights. The rate of inflation is 11.7 per cent, which is higher than

Table 2.1   Calculating a weighted average price index

Item	Weighting	Price rise (%)	Weighted price rise
Food	21	10	210
Alcohol	11	5	55
Housing	34	20	680
Clothing	11	10	110
Transport	23	5	115
	100	$\dfrac{50}{5} = 10$	$\dfrac{1170}{100} = 11.7$

the simple average price rise of 10 per cent because of the large rise in the price of the most important item, housing. The list of goods and services in the RPI or the CPI is obviously longer and the weights have to be revised from time to time to reflect changes in the spending patterns of the average household. For example, between 1975 and 1985 the average UK household spent a smaller proportion of its total budget on food, so the RPI weighting for food fell from 232 to 190.

In reality, there is no such thing as the average household. It is not simply that actual households exhibit different patterns of spending on, say, fuel and light. Many of these actual spending patterns are probably close to the average and where they diverge significantly for a particular group of consumers a special price index can be calculated. The average UK pensioner household spends a greater proportion of its total budget on fuel and light than the average for all households and so at times of rising fuel prices faces a different inflation rate from that shown by the RPI. The UK government therefore publishes a price index relating specifically to pensioner households.

The main difference between the RPI and the CPI concerns the measurement of housing costs, which is the most controversial aspect of the RPI. The existence of a substantial private rented sector in the US housing market makes it possible to use rents as a measure of housing costs in the CPI. However, the decline of the private rented sector in the UK housing market rules out this simple approach. The best measure of housing costs outside the council rented sector is taken to be the monthly mortgage repayment, on the grounds that this is the proportion of the monthly household budget that has to be allocated to housing. But the monthly mortgage repayment reflects the size of the capital sum borrowed to buy the house *and* the current rate of interest on that loan. Only the first of these items is related to the *price* of the house and then only after a time lag; a house that doubles in price in 1990 might have no effect on the RPI until it is sold in, say, 1995. Moreover, interest rates are more volatile than house prices and their impact on the RPI is almost immediate. Consequently, even a substantial rise in house prices, if accompanied by a fall in mortgage rates, might have no effect on the RPI. In 1987, for example, house prices rose by about 17 per cent but the housing item in the RPI actually fell because of lower mortgage rates. This undermines the accuracy of the RPI as a price index but enhances its reliability as a 'cost of living' index.

The answer to the question 'Which of these two things ought the RPI to be?' depends on the reason for wanting to know how quickly 'prices' are rising. If the purpose of ascertaining the rate of inflation is to inform a wage claim intended to maintain trade union members' standard of living, it is reasonable to consult the RPI because changes in mortgage rates are likely to have a greater impact on most people's current standard of living than changes in house prices. But if the intention is to gauge the underlying inflationary pressure in the economy or to compare the UK inflation rate with those of our industrial competitors, it makes sense in some circumstances to look elsewhere. For example, the Bank of England publishes a consumer prices index which is basically the RPI minus housing costs. However, a better measure of inflationary pressure in the economy as a whole is the gross domestic product (GDP) or gross national product (GNP) deflator.

GDP and GNP are alternative measures of the output of the whole economy, the economy being defined either as the factors of production located within the country's borders irrespective of the nationality of their owners or the factors of production owned by the country's citizens regardless of where they are used. GDP measures the value of the output produced within a country's geographical borders during a given period of time, while GNP measures the value of the output produced by domestically owned factors of production. The GDP/GNP deflator therefore reflects changes in the prices paid by firms for investment or capital goods and by the government for the goods and services it provides free to consumers as well as changes in the prices paid by consumers themselves. Table 2.2 shows the calculation of GDP in a hypothetical economy (with no government sector). Nominal or money GDP is found by multiplying the quantity of output by the prices for which it was actually sold. So nominal GDP in 1990 involves multiplying 1990 quantities by 1990 prices (£60 × 40 units for capital goods and £20 × 150 units for consumer goods). Nominal GDP has more than doubled since 1985 but some of this increase is due to inflation. How much can be found by calculating real GDP, which involves multiplying 1990 quantities by the prices prevailing in the base year, 1985 in this case (£50 × 40 units for

Table 2.2   Calculating the GDP deflator

	1985		1990		Nominal GDP		Real GDP	
					1985	1990	1985	1990
	Price	Quantity	Price	Quantity				
Capital goods	£50	20	£60	40	£1 000	£2 400	£1 000	£2 000
Consumer goods	£10	100	£20	150	£1 000	£3 000	£1 000	£1 500
					£2 000	£5 400	£2 000	£3 500

capital goods and £10 × 150 units for consumer goods). The GDP deflator is calculated as:

$$\frac{\text{Nominal GDP}}{\text{Real GDP}} \times 100 = \frac{5400}{3500} \times 100 = 154$$

This means that prices have risen by 154 per cent over the five-year period, giving an annual inflation rate of 31 per cent.

2.3   CONCLUSION

The RPI or the CPI and the GDP or GNP deflator are equally valid methods of measuring a persistent increase in 'the general level of prices'. The problem is that people do not want their incomes protected against the average or general rate of inflation but against the rate of inflation they actually face. When the poll tax was introduced in England and Wales in 1990, the UK government based its estimate of the rate it thought local authorities should set on the assumption that inflation had increased their expenditure by 4.64 per cent in the previous year. True, the UK GDP deflator had risen by 4.64 per cent. But the local authorities argued that their costs, mainly wages, had increased by about 8 per cent as workers sought compensation for the higher mortgage repayments reflected in the 'headline' RPI figures but not in the GDP deflator.

3. Explaining Inflation

3.1 INTRODUCTION

The aim of this chapter is twofold, comprising a straightforwardly expository purpose and a more ambitious polemical one. The first objective is simply to review the major explanatory theories of inflation, while the more ambitious one is to put forward a new interpretation of the inflationary process. Monetarist, demand pull, cost push and conflict theories of inflation will be examined to prepare the ground for interpreting the inflationary process as a *de facto* method of indexation. This perspective on the upward movement of the general level of prices has important implications for understanding the redistribution of income and wealth that tends to occur during periods of inflation (see Chapter 10).

3.2 MONETARISM

Throughout the 1980s macroeconomic policy in the UK and the US was based, with varying degrees of commitment, on the monetarist theory of inflation. Milton Friedman's proposition that *'inflation is always and everywhere a monetary phenomenon* in the sense that it is and can be produced only by a more rapid increase in the quantity of money than in output' (1991, p. 16) means that excessive growth in the money supply is the sole cause of inflation and implies that controlling that growth is its only cure. The root of monetarism is the quantity equation

$$MV = PY$$

where M = the money supply, V = its velocity of circulation or the number of times a unit of money changes hands during a given period of time, P = the average level of prices and Y = real national income or the quantity of goods and services produced during a given time period. The equation simply offers two ways of describing the same set of transactions. In a simple economy consisting of households and firms with no government and no investment, the amount of money spent by households when they buy goods is bound to be the same as the amount of money received by firms when they sell goods. In other words, the quantity of money multiplied by the number of times it is used to buy goods must equal the average price per good multiplied by the number of goods sold.

Two assumptions and one empirical relation transform the quantity equation into a theory of inflation. It is obvious that *if* in the extreme case V and Y were constant, any change in M would be accompanied by a similar change in P, and vice versa. So if it is assumed, for the sake of argument, that V and Y are constant, there would be a positive and directly proportional correlation between M and P. If M were to increase by 10 per cent, P would increase by 10 per cent, otherwise MV would no longer equal PY. In reality no one assumed that V and Y were constant but monetarists did draw attention to the empirical fact that both variables were stable, tending to change only rather slowly. The quantity theory recognizes the fact that a rise in M will cause both P and Y to increase but maintains that the dominant effect will be on P because the growth of Y is largely determined, not by short-term fluctuations in M and V, but by long-term trends in 'real' economic forces such as productivity. Friedman had no doubt that this prediction had been confirmed by many observations in widely different circumstances of an empirical relation between changes in the money supply and subsequent changes in the general level of prices.

There are two problems with monetarism. The first is the theoretical point that no correlation between M and P however strong is sufficient to establish a causal effect flowing from M to P. An obvious possibility is that changes in P are causing changes in M and not the other way round. In fact there appears to be a time lag between changes in M and subsequent changes in P but even this is not enough. If changes in M are followed by changes in P, the explanation could be that there is a third undiscovered variable which always accompanies M and is the actual cause of the changes in P or which causally affects both M and P.

Second, there is a practical problem in operating monetarist policy. It simply is not clear what should count as money in a modern economy. And this is important because until it is known what is to count as M it is impossible to measure and hence confirm the stability of V.

Money is a range of assets functioning as a more or less liquid store of wealth as well as a medium of exchange and it is impossible to identify a point along this spectrum where 'money' unequivocally becomes 'non-money'. In neither the UK nor the US is there a single official measure of the money supply. In the UK narrow money means M0 and M1. M0 is simply cash, that is, notes and coin in circulation with the public plus cash in the tills of the commercial banks and the cash balances they hold at the Bank of England. M1 consists of cash in circulation with the public plus sterling demand or 'checkable' bank deposits (those from which cash can be withdrawn on demand and against which cheques can be written). Broad money comprises M3, which is basically M1 plus sterling time bank deposits (those which earn interest), and M4, which is M3 plus building society shares and deposits but minus building society holdings of M3 to avoid double-counting.

The two officially targeted measures of the US money supply are M1 and M2. The US monetary authorities responded to financial innovation by expanding the narrow definition of the money supply to encompass the activities of thrift institutions (the US counterpart of building societies). Thus, M1 is a narrow definition comprising cash, demand deposits at commercial banks *and* checkable deposits at thrifts, while M2 equals M1 plus savings and small (less than $100 000) time deposits at both banks and thrifts. Broader monetary aggregates are M3, which adds large-denomination time deposits to M2, and L, which consists of M3 plus savings bonds and short-term Treasury securities.

When announcing its medium-term financial strategy in 1980, the Thatcher government chose to target sterling M3, as it was then known, because it appeared to be correlated with the RPI after an average time lag of 16 months. But the correlation broke down as the velocity of circulation of sterling M3 or 'broad' money fell by about 25 per cent with the consequence that in the mid-1980s M rose much faster than P. A somewhat similar velocity puzzle occurred in the US, where velocity was lower in 1985 than in 1980 after increasing steadily throughout the 1970s at an average rate of 3.5 per cent a year. This probably reflected the function of money as a liquid store of wealth rather than a medium of exchange; people were increasingly using the bank deposits for saving rather than as a way of financing current consumption. Greater competition in financial markets, as building societies offered cash dispenser and chequebook facilities on interest-bearing deposits, made it more difficult to draw the line between broad and narrow money. Having finally abandoned sterling M3 in 1987, in March 1988 the government announced a formal target for M0, which had continued to be quite closely correlated with the rate of inflation. But this statistical association appears to mean only that the transactions demand for cash changes as the inflation rate changes and does not signify a causal influence from a prior growth in M0 to a subsequent acceleration in inflation. In other words, if the goods which consumers are accustomed to buy increase in price consumers will need to carry more cash in order to continue to make their usual purchases.

US monetary policy in the 1980s evolved along broadly similar lines. In October 1979 the Fed (the US central bank) signalled a greater willingness to tolerate high interest rates in order to restrict the growth of M1 and M2 to target paths consistent with reducing an annual inflation rate of 13 per cent. However, both monetary aggregates have generally grown faster than their target range, even in the early 1980s when the economy moved into recession and the inflation rate fell below 5 per cent. So in both the US and the UK monetarist policies failed to restrain monetary growth but appeared to reduce inflation by precipitating recession.

The monetarist claim that excessive growth in the money supply is the sole cause of inflation and curbing that growth the only cure cannot be sustained. However, this does not mean that monetary growth has no place at all in the inflationary process. An increase in the money supply may be one indirect contributory factor among others in the generation of demand inflation. Instead of a direct effect flowing from M to P, from monetary growth to price rises, demand inflation may involve a causal process from monetary growth to excess aggregate demand (aggregate demand minus aggregate supply at prevailing prices) to price rises. While monetary growth may on some occasions be the dominant influence on the price level, on others it may play a purely accommodatory role as some other factor takes the lead in forcing up aggregate demand and hence prices.

3.3 DEMAND PULL INFLATION

Demand pull inflation occurs when aggregate demand (the total demand for goods and services in the various markets of the economy) exceeds aggregate supply (the total supply of goods and services) at prevailing prices. In Figure 3.1 the AD curve slopes downwards indicating that aggregate demand increases as the price level falls. But it is worth noting that the AD curve is not simply a large-scale version of an ordinary demand curve showing the quantities consumers are willing to buy at different price levels. For the AD curve incorporates changes in the money market as well as the goods market. If the price level falls, the quantity of real money balances increases; in other words the same amount of money will buy more goods. In real terms there has been an increase in the money supply, with the expected consequence that the rate of interest falls. This leads to an increase in borrowing by firms for investment and also by households for the purchase of consumer durables. Aggregate demand increases as the price level falls because the real money supply increases, lowering interest rates and stimulating investment and consumption.

An outward shift of the AD curve representing an expansion of aggregate demand normally affects both output Y and the price level P, the relative size of each effect depending on the slope of the AS curve. The AS curve is not linear but slopes upwards more steeply as the full employment level of output is approached. If firms wish to increase output when the economy is close to full capacity, they must offer higher rewards to attract scarce resources away from their current employment. So they are willing to increase output only if higher prices compensate them for the higher costs they face, a fact reflected in the steep slope of the AS curve. A demand expansion from AD^1 to AD^2 close to full employment is therefore largely inflationary in its impact with little effect on output (Figure 3.1). When the AS curve is almost flat, meaning that there is spare capacity in the economy, an expansion of aggregate demand from AD^0 to AD^1 quickly brings those

Figure 3.1   Demand pull inflation

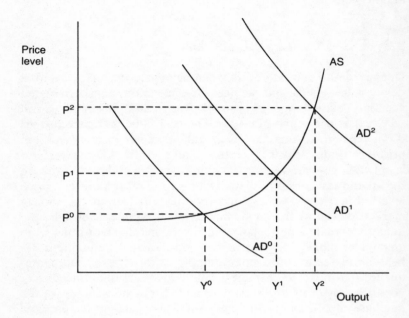

unemployed resources into play and output increases with little or no effect on the price level. Conversely, the flatness of this part of the AS curve means that a contraction of aggregate demand, shifting the AD curve to the left, is met by a fall in output rather than the price level. The explanation lies in the labour market.

The major part played by labour market processes in generating demand inflation gives rise to perhaps the most familiar relationship in macroeconomics, the inflation–unemployment trade-off. The original Phillips curve captured this relationship by plotting the rate of change of money wages against unemployment in the UK economy for the period 1861–1913 (Figure 3.2). These empirical observations implied a non-linear negative correlation between *wage* inflation and unemployment. Phillips explained the non-linearity of the relationship, specifically the fact that the curve is steep when the economy is close to full employment but fairly flat when unemployment is high, as the outcome of workers'

Figure 3.2   The Phillips curve 1861–1913

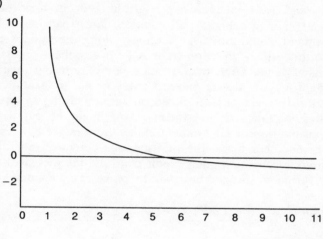

Rate of change
of money wages
(% per year)

Unemployment %

resistance to money wage cuts. Workers are unwilling 'to offer their services at less than the prevailing rates when the demand for labour is low and unemployment is high so that wages fall only very slowly' (Phillips, 1958, p. 283). In fact, an increase in unemployment from 4 per cent to 5 per cent is accompanied by no more than a fall in the rate of increase of money wages from 0.5 per cent to 0.1 per cent (Figure 3.2). On the other hand, a fall in unemployment from an already low 2 per cent to 1 per cent can be achieved only at the cost of an acceleration in the rate of growth of money wages from 2.8 per cent to 8.7 per cent. So the non-linearity of the AS curve is mirrored by that of the Phillips curve, meaning that demand inflation in the goods market is closely related to money wage inflation in the labour market.

The first development in what was to become the complicated evolution of the Phillips curve involved the substitution of price inflation for the rate of change of money wages, on the grounds that they are closely correlated. This is no coincidence; if prices are set as a mark-up on labour costs, price inflation can diverge from wage inflation only by the rate of change of productivity. The Phillips curve was immediately transformed into a map of the options facing macroeconomic policy makers, implying that monetary and fiscal policy measures are likely to be important factors in explaining demand pull inflation. An expansion of aggregate demand would move the economy along the Phillips curve in a north-westerly direction from A to B as policy makers accepted higher demand pull inflation as the cost of reducing unemployment (Figure 3.3). Lower interest rates or the relaxation of credit controls might be used to encourage borrowing to finance extra consumption and investment, taxes might be cut to stimulate consumption or government expenditure might be increased. If, on the other hand, the priority was to reduce inflation, higher interest rates or tighter credit controls, tax increases or cuts in government expenditure would move the economy along the

Figure 3.3   The Phillips curve

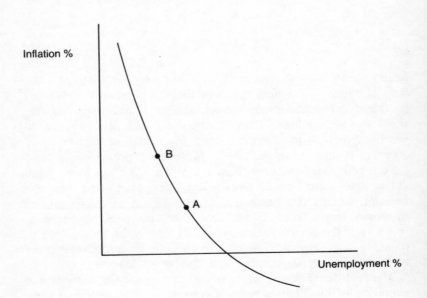

Phillips curve in a south-easterly direction, for example from B
back to A (Figure 3.3). Consumption and investment can also
increase independently of monetary and fiscal policy measures, if
for example consumers feel wealthier or business confidence
improves.

The evidence suggests that demand pressures have been instru-
mental in generating several episodes of inflation in recent years.
For the US, expansionary policies during the 1960s as government
expenditure increased to finance a social welfare programme and
to pay for the Vietnam war gave rise to a classic north-westerly
movement along the Phillips curve (Figure 3.4). But probably the
most spectacular episode of demand pull inflation in recent years
in either the UK or the US was the 'Lawson boom', so called after
the Chancellor of the Exchequer whose policy decisions were
largely responsible for it. The decision to abandon the target for
sterling M3 and cut interest rates to control the appreciation of
sterling permitted, while financial deregulation encouraged, an

Figure 3.4   The US Phillips curve 1960–89

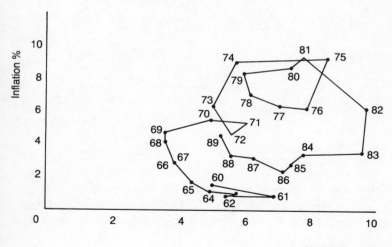

expansion in the money supply. Many people were willing to borrow more because house price rises and income tax cuts, particularly those in the 1988 budget, made them feel wealthier. The UK Phillips curve for 1986–88 shows the expected shallow north-westerly movement from a high unemployment base (Figure 3.5).

Figure 3.5   The UK Phillips curve 1970–90

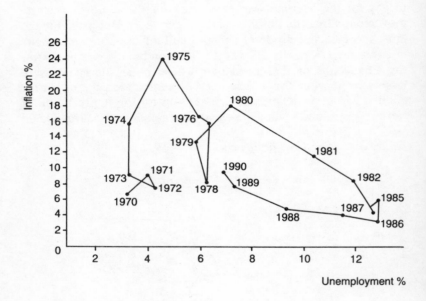

However, perhaps the most striking feature of UK and US Phillips curves in the 1970s is that the inflation rate accelerated most rapidly when unemployment was either constant or also rising.

3.4   COST PUSH INFLATION

Cost push inflation occurs when costs of production increase throughout the economy. The AS curve shifts upwards or to the left, implying a rise in the price level *and* a fall in output (Figure 3.6). So cost push appears in principle to be a reasonable explanation of the 1970s phenomenon of 'slumpflation', which combined higher inflation and rising unemployment. In so far as expansionary monetary and fiscal policies were used to shift the AD curve

Figure 3.6   Cost push inflation

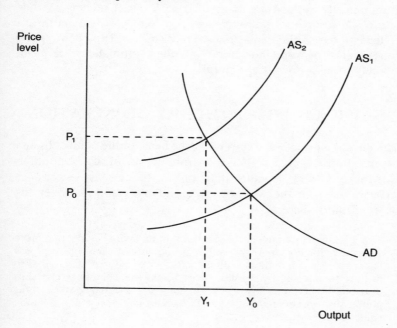

to the right by just enough to prevent the fall in output, accelerating inflation was associated with a constant rate of unemployment in a condition known as 'stagflation'. Either way, the Phillips curve shifts outwards, for example from PC^1 to PC^2 (Figures 3.4 and 3.5). It is obvious that the two oil price shocks shifted the UK and US Phillips curves outwards in 1974–75 and again in 1979–80.

What is less obvious is the relative importance of the part played by wages. Oil and labour have in common the fact that they are used in the production and distribution of virtually every good produced in the economy. The oil price rises occurred at a time when inflation was already on an upward trend, perhaps driven higher by 'wage pushfulness'. This involves money wage inflation initiated by some factor other than labour market pressure (for then it would be an aspect of demand pull inflation), such as trade union militancy, in an effort to increase the share of wages in national income or to protect workers' living standards in the face of price increases. In the US, COLAs or cost of living adjustments automatically compensate many workers for price increases, while in the UK compensation for rising prices tends to be a matter for collective bargaining and industrial disputes. Either way, the consequence of wage indexation, whether automatic or *de facto*, is likely to be a price–wage spiral.

3.5   THE CONFLICT THEORY OF INFLATION

The idea of a price–wage spiral is at the heart of the conflict theory of inflation. Using a Marxist framework of class conflict, Rowthorn (1977) explains inflation as the consequence of a struggle between the working class and the capitalists over the distribution of income.

> The working class can shift distribution in its favour by fighting more vigorously for higher wages, although the cost of such militancy is a faster rate of inflation, as capitalists try, with only partial success, to protect themselves by raising prices. Likewise, capitalists can shift distribution in their favour by pursuing a more aggressive profits policy, but workers fight back, so that once again the rate of inflation rises. (Rowthorn, 1977, p. 224)

The conflict theory can be seen as combining demand pull and wage push factors, either one being capable of instigating the inflationary process (or price–wage spiral) but the interaction of both being required for its development. Suppose that at a time of stable prices the government pursues expansionary fiscal and monetary policies in order to raise the level of aggregate demand. Capitalists seize the opportunity to increase the share of profits in national income by putting up prices. This redistributive goal explains why the extra demand feeds through into higher prices rather than greater output even though, it may further be supposed, there is spare capacity in the economy. Workers attempt to reverse the unfavourable redistribution of income by demanding higher wages, capitalists seek to maintain their redistributive advantage through further price rises and so it goes on. The inflationary process is under way, driven by conflict over the distribution of national income.

Of course wage push could be the prime mover of the process. A change in social attitudes might modify workers' perceptions of an equitable distribution of income, which prompts demands for higher wages. Anxious to avoid an increase in unemployment, the government expands aggregate demand and capitalists seek to reinstate the original distribution of income through higher prices. Either way the essential point of the conflict theory, as interpreted here, is that inflation occurs because conflict over the distribution of income provokes a wage–price spiral. Neither a once-for-all increase in prices by capitalists nor a once-for-all rise in wages is enough to sustain the persistent rise in the general level of prices that is inflation. Workers and capitalists must resist each other's aspirations through competing wage and price rises for the inflationary momentum to be maintained.

3.6 A REINTERPRETATION OF THE INFLATIONARY PROCESS

The purpose of this chapter is not simply to survey the principal theories of inflation but also to offer a radically different interpretation of the whole process. The core of this reinterpretation is the proposition that the consequence of wage indexation is a price–wage spiral. Two pieces of economic analysis (not widely perceived as complementary) can be used to construct a perspective for understanding the significance of this idea: Rowthorn's conflict theory of inflation and Friedman's advocacy of voluntary indexation. The assumption is that economic phenomena such as inflation are best understood as the unintended consequences of rational or utility-maximizing behaviour by households, firms and governments. So the essential insight of the conflict theory must be transplanted from the intellectual apparatus of dialectical materialism with its proletarian and capitalist classes to the world of orthodox economic analysis with its households, firms and governments. How is it possible for conflict to emerge in that world in such a way that it sustains the inflationary process?

The answer is suggested by Friedman's (1991) case for indexation. The basic principle of Friedman's argument is that beyond the limited sphere of public finance indexation should be voluntary. Compulsory indexation through legislation is recommended for taxation and government borrowing, on the grounds that people ought to be protected from the inflationary effects of politicians' decisions about public expenditure. Inflation makes it easier to raise the money for public spending through two forms of deception or disguise. First, income tax payers move into higher-rate bands or brackets as their salaries keep pace with rising prices. To solve this problem of fiscal drag or bracket creep, income tax brackets would be expressed in terms of, say, £1 000–£2 000 multiplied by a price index. Second, inflation reduces the real burden of government debt and hence its real value or purchasing power to the holders of that debt. It is much less of a sacrifice to repay £100 in 1991 than it would have been in 1961 but precisely for that reason that sum of money will not buy as many goods now as it would have done 30 years ago. So the face value of government securities would also be index linked to maintain their real value or purchasing power. Indexation of this kind could not be instant – because for example costs make it impractical to change tax brackets more than once a year at moderate rates of inflation – but it is universal in that all income tax payers or government bond holders benefit.

Beyond the compulsory indexation of public finances, Friedman's advocacy of the procedure is limited to suggesting ways in which voluntary indexation might be encouraged: 'I would leave it to the voluntary interests of people to engage in indexing and not try to enforce it in any way' (1991, p. 120). The obvious question is: Why not enforce indexing if it is so desirable? Friedman does not answer this directly but a reply is implicit in his comments on incomes policies, where he rejects a wage and price freeze on the following grounds: 'In the process you are preventing changes in *relative* prices and wages. . . . So you are introducing a whole series of *distortions* of a very considerable kind into your price structure' (1991, p. 126).

The result of instant and universal indexation would similarly be to keep relative prices and wages constant. This would be inefficient because the market allocation of resources would be distorted if relative prices were not free to vary in response to changing conditions of supply and demand. The implication is that voluntary indexation is better or more efficient than compulsory indexation precisely because it is *not* instant and universal. In so far as the degree of success economic agents have in seeking to index their prices or wages reflects the demand for and supply of the goods or services they provide, voluntary indexation is free of the distortions that vitiate the economic efficiency of price and wage controls.

Originally put forward in 1974, Friedman's recommendations have in part been implemented. It is the limited extent to which prices and wages and monetary transactions or contracts in general are compulsorily indexed that explains much of the inflation that occurs. And here is the essence of a reinterpretation of the inflationary process. Inflation itself, the persistent increase in the general level of prices, is not the problem but rather an attempted solution to the problem of unacceptable changes in the distribution of income. Actual inflation is the outcome of the best efforts that economic agents can make to pursue their own interests by voluntary indexation. And their interests in this context are defined in terms of the perceived redistributive effects of relative price changes. This model of the inflationary process can be illustrated by the following example.

Suppose that a monopolist increases the price it charges for the commodity it supplies. This in itself is not inflationary because it is only a single upward movement in the price of a single good and it might even be consistent with stable prices if at least one other price happens to fall sufficiently to offset the monopolist's increase. But there *is* a redistribution of income from consumers to the monopolist.

This redistributive effect of a change in relative prices is obviously not lost on consumers, who are themselves producers in markets exhibiting varying degrees of monopoly power. Naturally they try to reverse the redistribution by putting up the prices of their own goods, some of which are of course bought by the monopolist. If the monopolist was reflecting an increase in the relative scarcity of its product, the second-round price rises will not stick; consumers including the monopolist's household will be unwilling to pay them. These price rises will therefore be reversed, there will be no inflation and the original redistribution will remain intact. But what if the initial price rise by the monopoly producer overstated the greater scarcity of its product so that at least some of the second-round price rises are sustained? In that case the result is inflation – a rise in the general level of prices – and a partial reversal of the original redistribution that took place in favour of the monopolist. So the inflationary process has moderated the redistributive effect of the initial non-inflationary change in relative prices.

Inflation is therefore an unplanned and haphazard form of indexation, a spontaneous attempt to secure compensation for unwarranted changes in relative prices. The engine that drives the inflationary process is dissatisfaction with a change in the distribution of income caused by an opportunistic price rise. Any firm or household, or any organized or loose association of firms or households, may perpetrate the original price rise. Similarly, any other firm or household, or any organized or loose association of firms or households, may respond by competing price rises intended to reverse the redistributive impact of the first one. So the *causes* of inflation cannot be fully explained without an understanding of the putative redistributive *effects* of inflation.

The problem with the standard interpretation is the assumption that it is the inflationary process itself that redistributes in unplanned and undeserved directions. The force of this assumption derives from a comparison which is rarely made explicit between actual inflation and perfectly anticipated inflation. There is no doubt that income and wealth are redistributed during the course of an actual inflation and that this would not happen if inflation could be perfectly anticipated. But it does not follow that the redistribution of income and wealth was caused by inflation. The implicit assumption that underlies the fallacy that inflation causes a redistribution of income and wealth is that perfectly anticipated inflation which leaves relative prices unchanged is the normal state of affairs. If it were, actual inflation could legitimately be seen as a departure from the norm of constant relative prices, and the redistribution of income and wealth that occurs during inflation could reasonably be interpreted as the effect of inflation.

However, it is misleading to try to understand a real world inflationary process as a disturbance to relative prices that would otherwise be unchanged, as though perfectly anticipated inflation were normal. For inflation can be perfectly anticipated only if a system of instant and universal indexation is in place. It is not inflation that disturbs relative prices; inflation is the outcome of efforts to remove the disturbance. Inflation happens because economic agents attempt through voluntary indexation to restore the distribution of income that a relative price change has disturbed.

3.7 CONCLUSION

There is no single cause of inflation. The AD/AS analysis and the Phillips relationship provide perspectives for understanding each occurrence of inflation without implying that all inflations are generated and sustained by the same single force. Demand pull and cost push factors interact and, while excessive growth of the money supply is one of the demand factors, it is not always and everywhere the most influential one. The cast might be the same in each production but today's star might be tomorrow's walk-on part. Rather than the recurrence of a standard process, each inflation is a unique historical episode. If there is a common thread it consists in the spontaneous efforts of economic agents to secure compensation for what they perceive to be unwarranted changes in relative prices. In that case inflation is best understood as a form of partial indexation, undertaken by free individuals pursuing their own interests in markets of varying degrees of competitiveness.

4. Defining and Measuring Unemployment

4.1 DEFINING UNEMPLOYMENT

Unemployed people are those members of the labour force who are out of work. To be part of the labour force people must be of working age and fit and available for work. They must also want to work or be actively searching for work. People who choose to abstain from paid work are not unemployed, because they do not meet this last condition. The problem is how to distinguish such people from those who genuinely want to work but cannot find jobs. In the UK the number of people claiming unemployment benefit is counted, while in the US a survey is carried out among a representative sample of the population.

4.2 MEASURING UNEMPLOYMENT BY A CLAIMANT COUNT

The object of measuring unemployment is to discover how many people satisfy the two essential conditions of being without a job and being interested in finding work. In the UK the official unemployment figures are produced by counting the number of people claiming unemployment benefit (or income support after twelve months of continuous unemployment) on the assumption that these are also the people who are out of work and genuinely seeking a job. However, a claimant count can misrepresent the facts about the 'true' level of unemployment in two ways. Some people claiming unemployment benefits may have no intention of taking a regular job or may even be working in the black economy, in which case the official figures overstate the 'true' unemployment level. On the other hand, some people who are desperately seeking work may not be eligible to receive unemployment benefits, in which case the official figures understate the 'true' unemployment level.

The size of these two offsetting groups can be estimated, using data from the annual labour force survey conducted by the Department of Employment. In 1985 there were 800 000 people who were not claiming benefits but *were* actively searching for a job, while 990 000 were claiming benefits but were unavailable for work, were not actively searching for a job or were already in work. The net effect of adding the first group and subtracting the second was marginally to reduce the official figures from 3.13 million to 2.96 million. So at that time the official UK unemployment figures appeared to be approximately correct, if only as a result of a happy accident. But things have changed.

The main drawback with relying on a claimant count as a guide to the true level of unemployment is that it is vulnerable to administrative revision. Moreover, governments have two powerful incentives to change the regulations on eligibility for unemployment benefits in a way that is likely to underestimate the true unemployment level. Not only will they reduce the fiscal costs of unemployment by avoiding extra expenditure on benefits, they will also enhance their popularity with the electorate by cutting the 'headline' total. The Thatcher government made numerous changes to the eligibility conditions for unemployment benefits, all but one of which adjusted the official figures downwards. Job creation and training schemes which have also been developed are sometimes seen as attempts to remove their participants from the unemployment count rather than to provide 'real' jobs or worthwhile training.

The four most recent administrative revisions illustrate the controversy surrounding the reliability of the official unemployment figures. First, all 16–17-year-olds were removed from the count in October 1988 when their entitlement to unemployment benefit was withdrawn on the grounds that a place on a job creation or training scheme was available for every school-leaver. Second, by the end of 1987 new claimants faced a questionnaire on their availability for work, which was designed to discourage claimants who were not genuinely seeking a job. Third, at the same time the Restart programme required the long-term unemployed (those without work for twelve continuous months) to attend an interview and counselling sessions to encourage a more committed and effective approach to finding a job. Fourth, since 1989 unemployment benefits can be withdrawn from claimants who refuse reasonable job offers on the grounds that they offer lower pay than their previous employment.

It is clear that administrative changes have significantly affected the official UK unemployment count. The Unemployment Unit has produced an estimate of UK unemployment for January 1989 on the assumption that no administrative changes had been made since 1979 (Table 4.1). The percentage rate has been affected since 1986 by the decision to include the self-employed and the armed forces in the denominator.

Table 4.1   UK unemployment, January 1989

Official figures for UK unemployment	1 988 000	7.0%
Unemployment Unit estimates	2 678 900	9.4%

Source: Clark and Layard (1989), Table 2, p. 6.

An alternative way of producing a consistent series is to calculate unemployment for past years according to the current definition. When the Department of Employment carried out this exercise, the result was a significant downward revision of the unemployment figures for the 1970s. For example, in 1979 1.08 million people were unemployed, a third of a million fewer than were believed to be out of work at the time the general election was fought.

Although the Thatcher government has been severely criticized for supposedly 'fiddling' the unemployment figures, the allegations are based on the assumption that there was nothing wrong with the way the figures were being counted in the first place. In principle claimants had to establish their eligibility for benefit by convincing officials that they were available for work and were willing to work. But in practice all that was required was to complete a form which asked 'Would you take any job you could do?' Most claimants answered 'yes' and were immediately assumed to be available for work and hence eligible for benefit. If they refused offers of suitable employment they became liable to lose benefits for up to 13 weeks, and ultimately to prosecution.

But the operation of 'benefit stop' was very rare and the last section 25 prosecution was recorded in 1982. So there were reasonable grounds for tightening up the administration of unemployment benefits. In any case, from an international perspective some of the major changes, like the availability questionnaire and the Restart programme, were a 'catching-up' exercise, being broadly similar to reforms introduced as long ago as the mid-1960s in the US and in 1982 in France.

4.3 MEASURING UNEMPLOYMENT BY A LABOUR FORCE SURVEY

It is sometimes claimed that the only reliable method of measuring unemployment and the only valid basis for making international comparisons is the representative sample survey. But the results of a survey are notoriously sensitive to the assumptions and objectives of those who frame the questions, to the demeanour of those who put them to respondents and of course to the attitudes of the respondents.

In the US the official unemployment figures are collected by a monthly survey of a representative sample of the population comprising 47 000 households. Respondents are asked direct questions to establish whether they are unemployed in the sense that they are available for work, did not work for profit during the survey week and actively looked for work during the four weeks before the survey. Actively searching for work includes registering at an official agency, writing letters of application, placing and answering job advertisements and checking with friends and relatives.

Two problems are immediately obvious. First, there is no absolute and universal principle justifying the use of four weeks as the job search period. The Japanese unemployment survey stipulates one week, the Norwegian eight. This matters; when the UK labour force survey switched from one week to four, the measured unemployment rate increased by 10 per cent. Second, there is no unassailable answer to the question of what activities are to count as looking for work. Is the person who registers with an employment agency but never actually visits it really searching for a job? Does checking with friends or relatives express a genuine desire for work or is it merely 'going through the motions'?

This raises the most serious issue concerning unemployment surveys, which is that the answer 'no' to the question 'Have you looked for work during the last four weeks?' can reflect very different attitudes to work. Presumably the respondent is not interested in finding a job and has in effect opted out of the labour force. But why? Taken at face value the answer 'no' appears to be the voice of the work shy. But it became clear that in many cases it reflected the discouragement and even despair of those who had experienced repeated failure in their search for work and were not convinced that further endeavour held out a realistic chance of success. The US labour force survey has accordingly identified discouraged workers as a sub-group of those people who are outside the labour force. In 1986, when 8.2 million people were officially recorded as unemployed, 1 million people were recognized as discouraged workers. It is arguable that those discouraged workers should be added to the official unemployment figures. The problem remains that there is no uncontroversial criterion, independent of the interviewer's judgement, for discriminating between those who are unworried by the prospect of further idleness and those who are desperate for work.

The calculation of internationally comparable unemployment rates must begin with data from labour force surveys which have been carried out so far as possible in the same way. The Organization for Economic Co-operation and Development (OECD) publishes standardized unemployment rates based on surveys conducted in accordance with guidelines announced by the International Labour Organization (ILO) in 1982 (OECD, 1988). These figures are largely free of the distortions caused by national variations in registration data and survey methods. However, standardized unemployment rates are affected by institutional and cultural differences across countries, which undermine their reliability as a measure of capacity utilization.

4.4   UNEMPLOYMENT AND CAPACITY UTILIZATION

The principal reason for measuring unemployment is to obtain an indication of the level of capacity utilization. But even standard-ized unemployment rates are not invariably reliable indicators of resource utilization because they inevitably reflect differences in national labour market structures, policies and customs.

A 'star performance' in the international unemployment league table does not necessarily indicate a dynamic high-growth economy. In the first place, the fact that a slowdown in the growth rate of GDP is not matched by a rise in unemployment can be explained in some countries by the out-migration of foreign workers. Adjusting the official figures for the migration of redun-dant workers from Switzerland, West Germany and Austria back to their countries of origin during the period 1974–79 increases unemployment rates for 1979 by 3.2, 1.3 and 0.2 percentage points respectively. Second, there is the problem of the consistent treatment of special employment programmes and training schemes. In Sweden, for example, where job losses were met by the expansion of retraining schemes, low growth was accompanied by a fall of 0.4 percentage points in officially recorded unemploy-ment over the period 1974–79. Adding workers on such schemes to the official figures results in unemployment *rising* by 0.4 percentage points. But perhaps at least some of the programmes involved genuine retraining. Finally, in Japan firms are more likely than in other countries to hoard labour, while workers, especially part-time women factory workers, are more likely than elsewhere to leave the labour force when they lose their jobs. Adjusting the official 1975 unemployment rate of 1.9 per cent for job losers who withdrew from the labour force takes it up to 3 per cent.

4.5   CONCLUSION

There is no uniquely true unemployment figure any more than there is a single true inflation rate. The reason for wanting to measure unemployment determines which method is appropriate. A claimant count is obviously the basis for establishing the cost of unemployment benefit to the taxpayer. But its vulnerability to administrative revision severely reduces its utility as an indicator of wasted resources. There is no alternative to a labour force survey when it comes to using a measure of unemployment to gauge the extent of resource utilization. International comparisons can be misleading but the problems beset the 'star performers', and OECD standardized unemployment rates for the UK and the US appear to be largely free of distortion.

5. Explaining Unemployment

5.1 THE CENTRAL QUESTION OF UNEMPLOYMENT THEORY

Does unemployment just happen to people or do they more or less unwittingly bring it upon themselves? That is the central and simple question which theories of unemployment try to answer, albeit in ever more subtle and complicated fashion.

Three long-term trends can be discerned in the history of unemployment theory. In the nineteenth century economists of the so-called 'classical' school analysed unemployment as a temporary aberration in the working of the labour market. Their explanation of mass unemployment in the 1930s was that real wages were too high. Keynes, however, saw the cause of mass unemployment outside the labour market in a deficiency of demand in the goods market and he is generally agreed to have won the argument. But policy in the 1980s has been dominated by the ideas of conservative or new classical economists, who have returned to the assumption that the cause of unemployment is to be found in the labour market.

In terms of the central question, if unemployment is essentially a labour market phenomenon, it is always possible at least in principle for unemployed people to avoid it by modifying their behaviour, taking a wage cut or accepting an inferior job. If on the other hand unemployment arises in the goods market, there is nothing the unemployed can do to escape their predicament. They do not have the income to create the demand for goods that would in turn generate a demand for their labour. So the answer to the central question determines the appropriate policy response to unemployment. If unemployment is the consequence of labour market imperfections, the government's only responsibility is to legislate to alleviate these so that economic agents are free to solve their own problems. But if unemployment is the product of deficient demand in the goods market, it is up to the government to create incomes to generate the missing demand.

5.2   LABOUR MARKET EXPLANATIONS OF UNEMPLOYMENT

It is customary to divide unemployment into four types: frictional, structural, classical and demand deficiency. Placing them in this order is intended to reflect the degree to which they postulate departures from the operation of a perfectly competitive labour market. A possibly mythical nineteenth-century *laissez-faire* economist might be imagined to be willing to tolerate the idea of frictional unemployment, rather less willing to admit structural unemployment, and so on.

In microeconomic terms unemployment is the excess of labour supply over labour demand. In a perfectly competitive market there would be no involuntary unemployment at all, for whenever the conditions of supply or demand changed the price mechanism would operate automatically to return the market to equilibrium. In other words wages would fall immediately after an increase in labour supply or a decrease in labour demand until the quantity of labour supplied once again equalled the quantity demanded. In such a market any 'unemployment' that might be observed would be voluntary, in that anyone without a job could be presumed to have made a free choice in favour of idleness.

In the real world there might be a delay before the adjustment occurred. If every vacancy was instantly filled by an unemployed person, the labour market would be at point A (Figure 5.1). But labour market frictions prevent this. Unemployed people do not have perfect knowledge of all job vacancies and employers seeking labour may not know where to find suitable applicants. So the number of job slots actually filled falls short of the theoretically possible equilibrium. The curve EE, always slightly to the left of a possible intersection of labour supply and demand curves, shows the number of job slots actually filled for different labour market equilibria. Frictional unemployment is generally regarded as small scale and short term, lasting only until the newly unemployed person has had time to acquire knowledge of job vacancies.

Structural or mismatch unemployment occurs when the skills of

Figure 5.1   Frictional unemployment

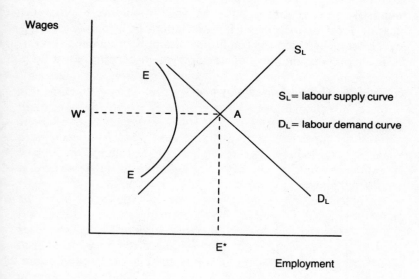

the unemployed are not the skills required by employers with job vacancies. Perhaps some unemployed people do have the appropriate skills but they are unable to move to the region where the vacancies exist. The occupational and geographical immobility which gives rise to mismatch unemployment are in effect more powerful labour market imperfections than the information deficiencies which account for frictional unemployment. There is a sense in which people can be thought of as bringing mismatch unemployment on themselves; in principle they could retrain or move to where the jobs are. But to the extent that the unemployed lack the income to sustain a private market in training there might be a major role for the government in providing training programmes. Moreover, geographical immobility might be the consequence of government intervention in the housing market. For example, the decline of the private rented sector in the UK housing market is one cause of the weak geographical mobility of labour compared to the US.

Classical unemployment is a microeconomic phenomenon but one which moves still further away from the assumption that the labour market is perfectly competitive. Trade unions use their monopoly power either to push the wage rate above the market-clearing level or to prevent it from falling to a market-clearing level after a change in the conditions of supply or demand (Figure 5.2). Or perhaps the level of unemployment benefits sets a floor

Figure 5.2   Classical unemployment

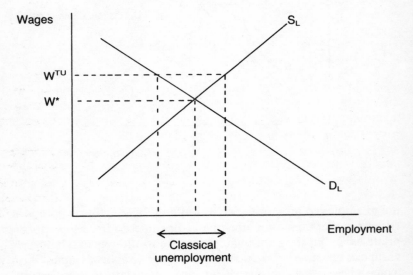

W^{TU} = wage rate negotiated by trade unions
W^* = equilibrium wage rate

beneath which wages cannot fall because no one will work when they can achieve the same income without working. Classical unemployment is also known as real wage unemployment. The wage rate that determines the demand for labour is the real product wage, that is, the money wage deflated by the price of the product that labour produces. If the real product wage rises throughout the economy some firms may be unable to cover their variable costs of production and will therefore close down. People bring classical unemployment on themselves in the sense that they choose to belong to organizations that prevent real wages from adjusting as necessary to clear the labour market. They are, as Conservative politicians like to say, 'pricing themselves out of jobs'. Or they may be choosing leisure subsidized by welfare benefits. Classical unemployment can be substantial and long term for it is reasonable to assume that a commitment to the principle of 'equal pay for equal work' makes it impossible to reduce wage rates to create jobs for the unemployed without cutting wage rates for those already in work.

5.3 AGGREGATE DEMAND DEFICIENT UNEMPLOYMENT

Keynes attacked the classical theory that unemployment occurs because real wages are too high and located the cause of the mass unemployment of the 1930s altogether outside the labour market. Keynesian or demand deficient unemployment arises because aggregate demand, the demand for the national output of goods and services, is so low that it can be met without employing all the people who want to work at the prevailing wage rate. In Figure 5.3 Y^{FE} is the full employment equilibrium level of national income; everyone who wants to work is needed to produce that output and the incomes generated in producing it give rise to a level of aggregate demand that is exactly sufficient to buy it. Suppose that AD^1 falls to AD^2, perhaps because businesses lose confidence in the future and cut back investment or the government reduces public expenditure in the fight against inflation. The new equilibrium level of national income, Y^U, will be too low to provide jobs for everyone who wants one, causing involuntary unemployment equal to $Y^{FE} - Y^U$.

The cure for Keynesian unemployment requires the government to increase aggregate demand to return AD^2 to AD^1 and Y^U to Y^{FE}. Without such a reflation firms could not sell the goods the unemployed could produce if they were taken on. The demand for labour is perfectly inelastic at the level of employment corresponding to Y^U. In other words, firms simply do not have a demand for the unemployed labour, which means that it would be pointless for unemployed people to offer to work for lower real

Figure 5.3   Keynesian unemployment

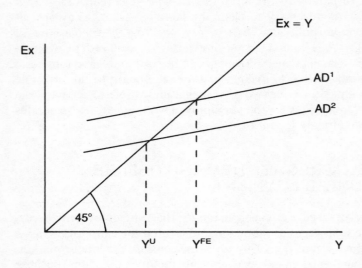

Ex = expenditure
Y = real national income

wages. There is no way in which the unemployed could be regarded as having brought their unemployment on themselves. However, while there is probably a consensus that Keynes was right about the 1930s, classical ideas about unemployment and the labour market were revived in response to the perceived failure of Keynesian policies in the stagflationary 1970s.

5.4   THE NATURAL RATE OF UNEMPLOYMENT

The natural rate of unemployment was defined by Friedman as the long-run equilibrium rate of unemployment which reflects the structure and institutions of the economy including such things as imperfections in the labour and goods markets, the cost of gathering information about job vacancies and the costs of mobility. So it can be seen as a way of gathering together the three labour market theories of unemployment: frictional, structural and classical. But the natural rate theory is more than that because it ascribes to economic agents a capacity for anticipating inflation in setting real wage targets, as a consequence of which the natural rate of unemployment cannot be reduced by a demand reflation.

The incorporation of inflationary expectations into labour market behaviour transformed the Phillips relationship and hence the policy options facing governments. According to Friedman, there is no long-run trade-off between inflation and unemployment; in the long run the Phillips curve is vertical. A moderate increase in inflation would reduce unemployment in the following way: a monetary expansion increases the demand for goods and hence causes a general price rise; nominal wages respond more slowly and the consequent fall in real wages induces firms to move down their labour demand curves; unemployed people, anticipating stable prices, are willing to work at the unchanged level of nominal wages and so unemployment falls. The economy moves north-west from A to B along PC^1 (Figure 5.4). This process depends on mistaken expectations about inflation. Once workers perceive the fall in real wages, they quit their jobs or negotiate for higher nominal wages. In either case unemployment returns to its original level while the new rate of inflation remains constant, shifting the Phillips curve from PC^1 to PC^2 as the economy moves from B to C. The government, having sought to reduce unemployment at the cost of a moderate rate of inflation, is soon confronted by the original rate of unemployment in combination with the induced higher rate of inflation.

In the long run there is no trade-off between inflation and unemployment and so the long-run or expectations-augmented Phillips curve is vertical at U^n. This is the natural rate of unemployment, that is, the rate of unemployment to which the economy tends to return whenever the rate of inflation is steady (and the expected and actual inflation rates are equal). Unemployment falls below the natural rate only if inflation is accelerating during each expansionary phase, so that expected inflation, which depends on past rates of inflation, is less than the actual rate. If the government reacts to this state of affairs by repeatedly expanding aggregate demand, inflation will accelerate while unemployment falls only temporarily.

Figure 5.4   The natural rate of unemployment

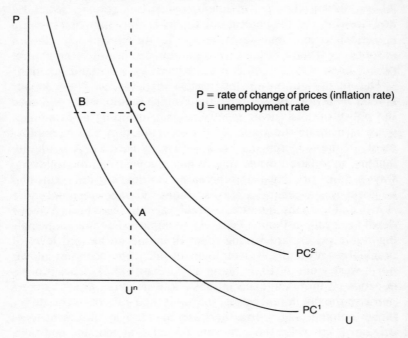

This idea of the natural rate of unemployment has been taken up, in one form or another, by most macroeconomists. The consensus is probably that it is possible to ride the short-run Phillips curve, using a positive demand shock to drive unemployment temporarily below the natural rate at the cost of accelerating inflation or a negative demand shock to reduce inflation at the cost of pushing unemployment above the natural rate. But this is only a short-run trade-off. The expectations-augmented Phillips curve, and with it the natural rate of unemployment, appears to have become firmly established in mainstream macroeconomics.

5.5   UNEMPLOYMENT IN THE UK AND THE US

It is obviously important to be able to estimate the natural rate of unemployment in order to answer the question 'How much of the unemployment at any particular time is natural and how much is demand deficient?' Measuring unemployment itself is so fraught with practical difficulties that a substantial margin of error is unavoidable (see Chapter 4). But in principle we could line up everyone in society and get from each person a truthful answer to the question 'Do you have a job and if not do you want one?' Measuring the natural rate involves an altogether more intractable kind of problem. We would have to divide people into employers and employees and ask them hypothetical questions about the terms on which they would be willing to employ or work for one another – in the light of assumptions, which may or may not prove reliable, about the actions of another group of people called the government. To measure the natural rate of unemployment is to guess the outcome of just such a gigantic bargaining process.

According to most estimates, which obviously compare in reliability to forecasts of next summer's weather in London rather than readings of today's temperature, the natural rate exhibits a long-term rise in both the UK and the US. In the US estimates of the natural rate put it at 3.5–4.5 per cent in the 1950s and 1960s, increasing to 4.5–5.5 per cent in the early 1970s and 5.5–6.5 per cent in the 1980s. Actual unemployment exceeded the natural rate by the widest margin during the recession of the early 1980s, when it rose from 5.8 per cent in 1979 to 9.7 per cent in 1982. This margin of demand deficient unemployment above the natural rate was a by-product of the monetarist experiment to eliminate inflation. A similar picture is observable in the UK, with one significant difference. Again there was a long-term increase in the natural rate and again actual unemployment rose well above the natural rate, from 4.3 per cent in 1979 to 9.9 per cent in 1982, as a consequence of the monetarist battle against inflation. The striking difference is the fact that actual unemployment went on rising long after the recession of the early 1980s was over, to peak at 11.3 per cent as late as 1986.

5.6 CONCLUSION

The mainstream answer to the central question is that unemployment above the natural rate is not something the unemployed have brought upon themselves and can be eliminated only by expansionary demand policies. But natural unemployment is a microeconomic labour market phenomenon and it can be reduced if economic agents such as trade union members and the unemployed adjust their aspirations and modify their behaviour, perhaps assisted by government legislative action to make the labour market more competitive.

PART II
The Costs of Unemployment and the Costs of Inflation

6. The Costs of Unemployment versus the Costs of Inflation

6.1 THE PUBLIC DEBATE ON THE COSTS OF UNEMPLOYMENT

The question of the damage that is done by unemployment raises deeply theoretical and highly controversial issues. Imagine two possible answers from people in the street to the question 'What is wrong with unemployment?' The answers would obviously reflect political beliefs. Those on the left might begin by remarking on the injustice of people being deprived of opportunities to earn a decent living and on the depression and even despair suffered by the unemployed. They might go on to claim that beating unemployment is in everyone's interest because national output could be higher if only the unemployed were enabled to do the work they desperately want to do. And they might add that even the most self-interested would gain from lower taxes. Conservatives, on the other hand, might begin by complaining of the injustice to hard-working taxpayers of having to subsidize the work shy. They might go on to claim that since the unemployed evidently prefer leisure to gainful employment there is no cause to feel sorry for them. And they might add that taxes could be lower and national output higher if unemployment benefits were to be withdrawn and the unemployed thereby obliged to fill the numerous vacancies employers constantly advertise.

These stereotypes illustrate a number of intuitions or hunches concerning the public debate about the costs of unemployment. First, it would probably be widely agreed that unemployment is a terrible waste; people who could and should be producing goods are not doing so. The costs of unemployment are immediately visible in derelict factories, decaying towns and empty lives. Second, there is much less agreement over the question of who is responsible for the waste – the unemployed who do not really want to work or the government for mismanagement of the economy. Third, most people probably feel that what is really wrong with unemployment is its unfairness. Fourth, where the two stereotypes might once again differ vehemently is over the question of who is being treated unjustly – the unemployed who are denied a chance to gain their fair share of material goods and make a contribution to society, or taxpayers who are coerced by the state into supporting the work shy.

6.2   A FRAMEWORK FOR INVESTIGATING THE COSTS OF UNEMPLOYMENT

Economic textbooks tend to assume that the question 'What are the costs of unemployment?' is simple enough to answer in principle. There is the obvious macroeconomic cost of losing the output the unemployed could have produced; there are the human costs of loss of income to the unemployed and psychological damage to them and their families; and there is the burden on taxpayers of having to finance unemployment benefits. The problem is the practical one of how to put a precise and reliable figure on these costs. But before examining some attempts to do this it is important to clear up a conceptual problem, a confusion concerning the way we think about the costs of unemployment.

The problem arises because it is natural to want to rank the perceived costs of unemployment in some sort of order of importance. Is the human cost a more or less serious problem than the output cost? This seems a perfectly reasonable question, although it is difficult to see how we can possibly compare such different things. In fact there is no reason to try to make this impossible comparison because the idea of ranking the costs of unemployment does not really make sense. It makes sense to rank, say, the West German, French and Italian economies in terms of output because the output of each national economy can be added to that of the others to find the total output of the three economies. But the output cost of unemployment cannot be added to the financial penalties it imposes on the unemployed and on taxpayers to give the total costs of unemployment.

When people lose their jobs society loses the output they would have produced had they remained in work. In a sense that is the only loss incurred through unemployment. For the loss of income suffered by the unemployed and the reduction in after-tax income experienced by taxpayers indicate how the burden or incidence of output loss is shared between the unemployed and taxpayers. Information about the financial loss to the unemployed and the fiscal costs of unemployment enables us to answer the question 'What difference does it make to people's lives that output is being lost?' The loss of goods that might have been manufactured but were not and never will be is a failure to realize potential and hence a somewhat abstract or hypothetical deprivation compared to the confiscation of actually existing goods from those who had become accustomed to enjoying them. Yet this loss of potential output does have serious effects on people's well-being. People's actual incomes here and now are lower than they otherwise would be, either because they have lost their jobs or because they are paying higher taxes.

The main cost of unemployment to the economy as a whole is the loss of potential output. The loss of income to the unemployed and the loss of after-tax income to taxpayers are not additional costs to be ranked in order of importance; they indicate the incidence of output loss. This is not to say that there are no other costs of unemployment. There *are* extra costs. These are the effects of losing a job on the mental and physical health of unemployed people and possibly the consequences of the aberrant behaviour of some of them on other members of society.

6.3 ANTICIPATED AND UNANTICIPATED INFLATION

There is a secure foundation from which to start in measuring the costs of unemployment: output that might have been produced is not in fact being made. True, it is not long before complications and controversies are encountered but at least it is clear that if potential workers are not working, obviously and necessarily goods that might have been made are not being produced. The main problem in investigating the cost of inflation is that it is not *obviously and necessarily* related to output loss or to any other effect on the real economy of work and consumption. If the general level of prices is rising persistently, obviously and necessarily . . . what? The answer seems to depend on who you are. There are several different ways in which inflation is claimed to be bad for us, most of them involving quite complex chains of cause and effect, and there is no general agreement on which is the most serious kind of inflationary damage.

Why do ordinary people worry about inflation? Not all of them do. Someone buying a house on a mortgage in the UK might be justified in wanting more inflation to reduce the burden of the debt. Price rises are usually accompanied by wage rises, and a few years of moderate inflation can soon make mortgage repayments taking say half a salary reduce to only a fifth of it. So the rise in consumer prices is matched by wage rises and the real burden of debt is reduced, provided inflation is anticipated, that is, matched by wage rises. But what if inflation is even more comprehensively anticipated, as it would be if lenders demanded higher interest rates? Inflation would then, as Wittgenstein said about philosophy, 'leave everything as it is'.

So the first principle of estimating the costs of inflation is that inflation really matters only to the extent that it is not anticipated. In so far as a correct inflation forecast is incorporated into the decisions taken by households and firms, inflation leaves everything as it is in real terms. Price rises are accompanied by equivalent increases in money incomes, so the cost of living is unchanged. Of course, in practice inflation is never *perfectly* anticipated and so there is scope for it to affect the welfare of people whose money incomes are not keeping up with price rises.

6.4   DOES INFLATION ROB THE RICH TO PAY THE POOR?

Unless it is perfectly anticipated, inflation creates winners and losers, people with money incomes which increase by at least as much as inflation and those whose money incomes fail to rise in step with inflation. In other words, inflation, because it is always to some extent unanticipated, redistributes income in various directions, depending on the speed with which different social groups react. Obviously the most serious losers are people on fixed money incomes, such as UK old age pensions before they were indexed to the RPI.

Perhaps the simplest example of income redistribution under inflation concerns debtors and creditors. To the extent that inflation is unanticipated and therefore not embodied in the rate of interest, debtors win and creditors lose. If Mr Loser lends Mr Winner £100 for one year at a 10 per cent interest rate and prices rise by 20 per cent during that year, then Mr Loser has effectively *given* Mr Winner £10. Mr Winner has paid a total price, including the cost of credit, of £110 for goods which, had he saved up for them, would have commanded a cash price at the end of the year of £120. The £110 which Mr Loser is repaid by the end of the year will not buy the goods he could have purchased with the £100 he chose to lend at the start of the year.

Inflation might also alter the distribution of national income between wages and profits. For example, the initial effect of demand pull inflation is to drive prices up, increasing profit margins and the cost of living before wages respond. So demand pull inflation tends to raise the share of profits in national income at the expense of wages. On the other hand, when cost push inflation is set in motion by wage rises, profit margins shrink before prices are increased so the share of wages in national income increases.

Inflation might redistribute wealth as well as income. Real assets such as works of art, antiques, and sometimes even houses, which are in limited supply tend to rise in price more rapidly than most goods and services. Owners will therefore find that the purchasing power of their wealth has actually increased during inflation.

The redistributive impact of inflation is the net outcome of these effects on the recipients of fixed incomes, on debtors and creditors, on workers and shareholders and on the owners of real assets. This is difficult if not impossible to assess, because an individual might be a loser as a creditor but a winner as an owner of a real asset whose relative value has appreciated. All that can be said with confidence is that inflation redistributes income and wealth away from people who do not anticipate it towards those who do. In any case even perfectly anticipated inflation is claimed by some people to have real effects.

6.5   IN SEARCH OF THE OUTPUT COSTS OF INFLATION

Who are these people who believe that even if every price rise were to be matched by a money income rise, leaving real incomes and hence living standards unchanged, there would still be effects on the real economy of output and jobs? They are of course economists. Two standard arguments appear to be widely accepted in principle, although there is some disagreement about the magnitude of the effects involved, known as shoe leather costs and menu costs. Shoe leather costs represent the resources consumed in making frequent trips to the bank in order to withdraw cash. The reason for this behaviour is that the purchasing power of cash is eroded by rising prices, so it makes sense to keep as much of one's income as possible on deposit in the hope of earning enough interest to keep up with inflation. In the extreme people would go to the bank several times a day to withdraw just enough cash for the transactions expected in the next few hours. It is clear that menu costs are incurred even during a perfectly anticipated inflation, because they are the resource costs of adjusting prices, such as the labour and materials used up in reprinting menus, price lists and catalogues, resetting vending machines and so on.

These arguments might appear to be somewhat far-fetched when the practical difficulties inflation is alleged to cause the business community are considered. The most urgent complaint of business leaders, certainly in the UK, is not in fact against inflation as such but against *relative* inflation, that is, a higher rate of inflation than those of other countries which sell the same goods on world markets. The danger is that sales of UK goods will fall as consumers switch to cheaper foreign goods. Industrial output in the UK will fall and jobs will be lost. This is a clear argument apparently based on the practical realities of commerce but it always pays to be suspicious of claims made by a particular interest group. Perhaps the real attraction of low inflation to business leaders is that it makes life easier for them – at the expense of some other group 'n any case, all that is required to solve the problem is to reduce the rate of inflation towards that prevailing in the UK's industrial competitors, not to eliminate it. There is no argument here for stable prices, unless zero inflation has already been achieved in the other trading countries.

The next argument seems to have a special appeal to economists who are enthusiastic in their advocacy of the free market. The claim is that markets cannot allocate resources efficiently unless prices are stable. The whole point of the market is that it is a forum where information is provided by changes in *relative* prices. In a competitive market economy rising prices and hence short-run supernormal profits in one industry attract new entrants from industries where prices and profits are flat or falling. In this way price changes move resources towards the production of the goods and services consumers most want to buy. Inflation inhibits the smooth operation of this process by making it difficult to pick out a change in relative prices indicating a switch in consumer preferences from the upward trend of prices in general. If price changes are signals of relative scarcity, inflation causes 'noise' or interference which distorts their clear transmission. Firms will make mistakes in responding to price signals and resources will be allocated in ways that do not accurately reflect the changing pattern of consumer preferences. When goods are produced for which there is no demand, stocks remain unsold, production is curtailed and jobs are lost. So even moderate inflation can cause unemployment.

6.6   DOES INFLATION *CAUSE* UNEMPLOYMENT?

The competitiveness and the inflationary noise arguments contain the germ of a crucially important idea, summed up in the words of former British Prime Minister, Harold Wilson: 'Inflation is the mother and father of unemployment.' If this claim is true, the consequences are dramatic. It implies a short answer to the question whether the costs of inflation are greater than those of unemployment. Of course they are, they must be as a matter of logic. In so far as inflation 'is the mother and father of' – that is, *causes* – unemployment, the costs of unemployment are simply the indirect costs of inflation. Inflation causes unemployment, which involves output loss, an inequitable redistribution of income and a deterioration in the psychological well-being of the unemployed. The root of these costs of unemployment is inflation. The competitiveness and the inflationary noise arguments imply that moderate inflation causes some output loss and hence unemployment. There is another line of thought which conservative or 'new right' economists and politicians have advanced in favour of the proposition that inflation causes unemployment.

This argument is sometimes offered by Conservative politicians as the justification for tolerating increased unemployment as the price that has to be paid for defeating inflation. Better a limited and temporary rise in unemployment now, they suggest, than the economic and social chaos that would occur in the future if inflation is not beaten once and for all. For the thing about moderate inflation, so they claim, is that it does not stay that way but exhibits an inexorable upward trend towards the ultimate catastrophe of hyperinflation and with it mass unemployment and total economic collapse. Indeed it was a commonplace of the inflationary 1970s that no democratic government had long survived an inflation rate of 30 per cent.

The idea that moderate inflation is somehow inherently liable to accelerate, and unless checked will ultimately turn into hyper-inflation, grew out of the introduction of expectations into the Phillips relationship or trade-off between unemployment and inflation. It will take several chapters to try to disentangle the complicated web of theories and evidence surrounding this issue.

6.7 CONCLUSION

Two comparative hypotheses can be put forward in order to provide a framework for investigating the costs of unemployment and inflation, one concerning their output costs and the other their redistributive and other welfare effects.

First, unemployment involves the *certainty* of substantial output loss now, while inflation involves the double *risk* of substantial output loss now and complete economic breakdown in the future.

Second, unemployment involves the certainty of redistribution away from the poor and imposes a severe psychological burden on some of the unemployed, while inflation redistributes income and wealth away from people in any income group or social category who do not anticipate it.

How much truth is there in these initial impressions? It is the task of the following chapters to answer that question and then to trace the implications of the answer for the central question of this whole inquiry: Which is the more serious problem – unemployment or inflation?

7. The Output Costs of Unemployment

7.1 THE SIZE OF THE PROBLEM

There is no consensus among economists about the size of the output loss associated with unemployment. According to Matthews and Minford (1987, p. 88), a registered UK unemployment rate of 11.7 per cent represented a waste of about 2 per cent of GDP. Junankar (1985), using Okun's (1970) methodology, estimated the output loss contingent upon a similar rate of UK unemployment in 1983 to be no less than 13.7–17.2 per cent of GDP. This study is particularly interesting because four methods of calculating the output cost of unemployment were used. The one that is closest to the average product approach which forms the basis of Matthews and Minford's estimate yielded an output loss of 8.5–10.0 per cent of GDP in 1983. For the US, the output gap, which is the amount by which actual GNP falls short of potential GNP, was 8.1 per cent of GNP in 1982 when the unemployment rate was 9.6 per cent (Dornbusch and Fischer, 1987). Yet Okun (1962) estimated that a 1 per cent rise in the unemployment rate would be accompanied by a 3 per cent fall in national output. So there is a wide variation in estimates of the elasticity of national output with respect to a change in unemployment. For the UK, it might be anything from 0.5:1 if Matthews and Minford are right to 1.5:1 on Junankar's highest estimate. In the US, Okun's original result of 3:1 has in effect been revised downwards to approximately 1:1 by Dornbusch and Fischer.

Two sources of disagreement explain much of the variation in these estimates. The first concerns the question of whether all unemployment is associated with output loss or whether there is a category of unemployment which is costless. The standard view is that only involuntary unemployment incurs output loss. Thus, Okun's (1962) 3:1 ratio of output loss to unemployment applied only to cyclical or demand deficiency, and hence involuntary, unemployment, while the 0.5:1 ratio implicit in Matthews and Minford (1987) excludes the allegedly voluntary element in unemployment by referring to *welfare* loss defined as output loss *net* of leisure (and black economy activity). An inquiry into the output cost of unemployment must therefore begin with an examination of the distinction between voluntary and involuntary unemployment. In this chapter it will be argued that this distinction is not identical with that between costless and cost-incurring unemployment. An alternative definition of costless unemployment, but one which is still based on commonsense descriptive categories, will be put forward and used to assess the assumptions underlying empirical estimates of the output costs of unemployment. Much of the chapter will therefore be concerned with the problem of deciding what part of total unemployment should be regarded as cost-incurring.

That leaves the second source of disagreement, which concerns the less intractable problem of measuring the output loss associated with that part of total unemployment which it has been decided to regard as cost-incurring. The choice here is between relatively crude methods such as multiplying the average product of the labour force by the number of unemployed and Okun's more sophisticated procedure for measuring the output gap. None of these methods of calculating the output cost of cost-incurring unemployment is perfect, so a not intolerably wide range of estimates of output loss is the only realistic goal. It will be concluded that the order of magnitude of the output costs of unemployment, if not their precise value, can be measured with a reasonable degree of reliability.

7.2 VOLUNTARY AND INVOLUNTARY UNEMPLOYMENT

It is clear that an estimate of the output costs of unemployment should not be based on a calculation of the amount by which national output would increase if *all* the unemployed were immediately to return to work. The assumption that unemployment could ever be reduced to zero is unrealistic. There will always be some frictional unemployment because real world labour markets cannot provide perfect information about vacancies and the skills of the unemployed. Frictional unemployment of this kind, which simply reflects the fact that labour markets are not paradigm cases of the perfectly competitive markets of textbooks, does not involve any output loss in comparison with any actually attainable state of full employment. If in the real world there is an irreducible minimum level of unemployment, it must be regarded as costless because no output that *could* be produced is being lost. In fact, some people may be frictionally unemployed because they are looking for better jobs than the ones they have left. If so, their unemployment is not merely costless; it might actually improve the efficiency of the economy by enabling people to find jobs which make full use of their skills. Finally, the concept of frictional unemployment is commonly extended to include people who, although they are seeking work, are effectively unemployable. No potential output is lost through failing to employ the unemployable, so such unemployment is again costless. The classification of frictional unemployment as costless is therefore uncontroversial.

The question of whether voluntary unemployment should also be regarded as costless is similarly uncontroversial in the literature. It will be argued that in this case the consensus view is mistaken. A natural assumption is that we can estimate the output costs of unemployment without knowing what its causes are: if resources are idle, production will be lower than it would be if they were in use. Surely, it might be thought, output is lost regardless of how the resources came to be left idle. The problem with this argument is that some or all of the unemployment might be voluntary in the sense that the unemployed derive greater utility from their leisure than from the earned income they could command if they chose to work. So their unemployment involves no net loss of utility at all but rather reflects a choice about the balance between leisure and goods as sources of utility. In principle, it follows that the costs of unemployment should include only the lost output of the involuntarily unemployed. The implication of this is that any estimate of the output cost of unemployment depends crucially on a judgement about how much of the actual unemployment observed at a particular time is voluntary and how much is involuntary.

The claim that voluntary unemployment is costless is clearly not true in the unqualified sense that it imposes no output costs *whatsoever* on society. If people are unemployed through choice it may be presumed that their increased leisure offsets their loss of income. But the income they lose is of course their income *net of taxes* and this is less than the value of their contribution to national output, their marginal product. The value of what people produce is equivalent to their *gross* income, some of which is taken by the rest of society in income taxes. So society *does* lose something when people become voluntarily unemployed; it loses that part of the value of their output that would have been taken in income taxes. The extra leisure the voluntarily unemployed enjoy compensates them for their private loss of income but it does not make up for society's loss of part of their marginal product. Voluntary unemployment certainly does not cost society as much lost output as involuntary unemployment but there is *some* loss of output. For example, on an income tax rate of 25 per cent, involuntary unemployment causes three times as much output loss as voluntary unemployment. So it still appears to be necessary to estimate the extent to which unemployment is voluntary.

This simply is not possible without making arbitrary assumptions. The voluntariness of a decision is a matter of degree. Coddington (1983, p. 31) distinguishes four ways in which unemployed people might become re-employed: by lowering their aspirations about the kind of work they are willing to do or the wage they are willing to work for; by acquiring new skills; by intensive search; or by becoming self-employed. People are voluntarily unemployed *to the degree* that they refuse to consider or fail to explore these four routes back to employment. But whether it is reasonable to expect people to accept a wage cut or a low-status job, to retrain or to set up their own businesses depends on their circumstances. Most young single people or childless couples can afford to be more flexible about these things than older people with family responsibilities. No feasible set of criteria for demarcating voluntary unemployment would be able to remove doubts about the classification of the numerous borderline cases that would inevitably exist. So there is no prospect of being able to isolate some proportion of total unemployment as unequivocally voluntary and hence much less costly in terms of output loss.

At this stage of the argument it appears that voluntary unemployment, while not entirely costless, causes only a fraction of the output loss involved in involuntary unemployment. The problem is that voluntary and involuntary unemployment cannot reliably be distinguished. If some unknown proportion of unemployment entails much less output loss than the rest, how can we estimate the output cost of unemployment?

7.3   COSTLESS AND COST-INCURRING UNEMPLOYMENT

A solution to this problem can be found by examining the assumption that, apart from that part of the voluntarily un-employed person's output that society takes in income taxes, voluntary unemployment is costless because the loss of goods is compensated by the gain in leisure. The existence of the poverty, or unemployment, trap makes it clear that unemployment which many people would regard as voluntary may nevertheless be cost incurring. The general principle informing this argument is that unemployment is cost incurring unless the unemployed (i) have in effect permanently withdrawn from the labour force or were never really part of it, or (ii) are in fact working in the black economy.

This principle can be applied to the descriptions of unemployed people used in a survey carried out among a representative sample of the UK population to elicit information about unemployed people personally known to them (see Table 7.1). The people in category B appear to constitute a paradigm case of voluntary unemployment in that, being better off on the dole, they must be presumed to have chosen to live on unemployment benefits rather than take the low-paid work which is all that is available to them. However, the people in this category may be deeply dissatisfied with their condition. When the alternatives are so limited that the one preferred would be undesirable to the majority of the popula-tion it is unreasonable to regard its selection as anything but reluctant. Nevertheless, a reluctant choice from limited alterna-tives is still a choice and so there is a sense in which the people in the poverty trap are voluntarily unemployed. The concept is ineradicably ambiguous. What *is* clear is that such unemployment is certainly not costless.

The emergence of the poverty (or unemployment) trap is an unintended consequence of the tax and social security systems.

Table 7.1   Categories of unemployed

Category	Number of people	Percentage of unemployed
A Genuinely unemployed	900 000–1 000 000	29
B Poverty trap	500 000–600 000	17
C Older workers 'retired on the dole'	350 000–450 000	12
D Unemployable	320 000–420 000	11
E Black economy	250 000–350 000	9
F Manage quite well on benefits	210 000–290 000	8
G Living off redundancy pay and benefits	210 000–290 000	8
H 'Holidaying on the dole' between jobs	100 000–200 000	5
I Drawing unemployment benefits while self-employed	up to 100 000	2
Total		101

Note: Those in category C are further described as having no intention of looking for work, those in category D as having stopped looking for work and those in category G as not looking for work.

Source: Opinion Research and Communication (1986), pp. i–ii.

Voluntary unemployment is one symptom of the disincentive effects that sufficiently high marginal rates of income tax can have on certain groups of people. The victims of the poverty trap have not permanently withdrawn from the labour force, in that reform of the tax and benefit system to remove or alleviate its unintended disincentive effects would be enough to persuade them to return to employment. The associated unemployment therefore imposes costs, irrespective of whether it is voluntary or involuntary on the part of the individuals involved, because the unplanned creation of the poverty trap deprives society of the labour of people who are capable of working and were never intended to be without employment. 'Voluntary' unemployment does not reflect a *collective* choice to take more leisure, and so the loss of output cannot be regarded as being offset by the gain in leisure. From a societal perspective, unemployment that might be voluntary on the part of the unemployed individual nevertheless incurs output costs.

What about the other categories? Those in categories F, G and H most closely approximate to the description 'voluntarily unemployed' and so there is a *prima facie* case for regarding their unemployment as costless. However, in so far as they remain unemployed because social security benefits provide a tolerable standard of living, their unemployment must be adjudged to incur costs on the grounds that were appealed to in connection with category B. The only difference between these people and those in the unemployment trap is one of degree: benefits erode the financial incentive to work rather than actually create a financial incentive to stay idle. Obviously, the unemployment of people in category A is both involuntary and cost incurring. The older workers and the unemployable in categories C and D would probably, and justifiably, resent the label 'voluntarily unemployed' but it is clear that their unemployment is costless. The people in category C have effectively left the labour force, while those in category D are frictionally unemployed. As for the people in categories E and I, they are evidently not unemployed at all, since they work in the black economy.

This interpretation of the survey results suggests that in the mid-1980s, when officially recorded UK unemployment was fairly stable at just over 3 million people, there were 1.92–2.38 million people in categories A, B, F, G and H whose unemployment, of whatever degree of volition, imposed costs on society. That leaves the 1.02–1.32 million people in categories C, D, E and I whose unemployment, again of whatever degree of volition, was costless. Of course, the results of one survey do not provide sufficiently robust evidence to support the general statement that about one-third of unemployment is costless. The point is simply that the definition of costless unemployment in terms of commonsense descriptive categories amounts to a criterion against which to judge assumptions about the proportion of unemployment to be excluded from empirical investigations into its output costs.

7.4 COSTLESS UNEMPLOYMENT IN EMPIRICAL ESTIMATES OF OUTPUT LOSS

A significant fraction of unemployment, it has been argued, does not entail any loss of output. Such costless unemployment takes three forms. First, there is frictional unemployment, the irreducible level of unemployment which occurs because of informational deficiencies in labour markets. Second, unemployment is costless to the extent that people officially counted as unemployed have effectively left the labour force or were never really part of it. This comprises the older workers who have 'retired on the dole' and the unemployables. Third, costless employment occurs when people officially counted as unemployed are in fact working for others or are self-employed in the black economy.

The standard approach to excluding costless unemployment from the measurement of output loss is based on the familiar point that full employment is not equivalent to zero unemployment. The feasible full employment baseline is then estimated and all unemployment in excess of the chosen figure counted as causing output loss. The question is whether this approach is likely to exclude from the calculation of output loss all and only the three categories of costless unemployment that have been identified.

Okun (1962) took the actual US unemployment rate in 1955 as his full employment baseline on the grounds that that was the year in which actual GNP was identical with trend GNP. The 1955 unemployment rate of 4 per cent was therefore accepted as the official full employment target. Since then changes in the composition of the US labour force have led to an upwards revision of the full employment estimate. Young workers and women workers change jobs frequently and so their greater importance in the labour force has increased frictional unemployment. Accordingly, the official full employment rate was revised to 6 per cent in the early 1980s (Dornbusch and Fischer, 1987, p. 11). It is clear, then, that Okun's approach correctly excludes frictional unemployment from the measurement of output loss. No allowance has been made for 'early retirements on the dole' but US welfare benefit arrangements, the relatively low incidence of unemployment among white males and the fact that unemployment is much higher among the young than among the older make it unlikely that this is a significant omission. However, the lack of any correction for black economy participation introduces a possibly significant upward bias in the measurement of output loss.

The most straightforward way of estimating the feasible full employment baseline is to take the lowest actual unemployment rate over a recent period of years as the closest feasible approximation to full employment. For example, UK unemployment in the early 1980s is measured by Junankar (1985) against unemployment during two previous periods, 1968–73 and 1974–79, one before and one after the first oil price shock. Using the high average unemployment of 1974–79 as a full employment proxy yields a low estimate of output loss, while the low average unemployment of 1968–73 produces a high estimate of output loss. The low estimate based on the 1974–79 full employment baseline seems preferable, if only because it approximately offsets the omission of black economy activity from the estimate of costless unemployment. Junankar's argument in defence of this procedure is simply an affirmation of the common assumption that in so far as 'higher unemployment was caused by increased social security benefits, the unemployment is voluntary and therefore has no costs' (1985, p. 18). Nevertheless, believing that the 'main reason for the growth in unemployment is . . . a lack of effective demand' (ibid.), Junankar counts all unemployment in excess of the 1968–73 or 1974–79 feasible full employment baseline as cost incurring. In terms of the threefold definition of costless unemployment, Junankar's approach correctly excludes from the measurement of output loss the frictionally unemployed and those who are effectively outside the labour force, but incorrectly includes those who are active in the black economy. Other things being equal, the results are therefore likely to overstate the output costs of unemployment, although only by 11 per cent if the ORC (1986) survey figures for black economy involvement are accepted.

On the face of it, the approach adopted by Matthews and Minford (1987) approximates to the threefold definition of costless unemployment. Starting from a registered unemployment rate of 11.7 per cent, they initially reduce it to 10 per cent by excluding those who are not really part of the 'available' labour force. The criterion of availability is ineligibility for unemployment benefits, on the grounds that the people concerned 'are not unemployed because of any market distortion, so that no available policy measure could draw them into employment in a welfare-improving way' (1987, p. 87). This appears to be an equally valid alternative way of operationalizing the idea that unemployment is costless if the unemployed have effectively left the labour force or were never really part of it. Their next step, to subtract 'some frictional rate', is uncontroversial in principle but no details of the estimate of frictional unemployment are offered. Matthews and Minford go on to recognize the need to revise the estimate of output loss downwards to take account of part-time activity in the black economy. But not only is no detailed justification for the size of the revision offered, it is not even separately quantified (ibid., p. 88). So far, Matthews and Minford's approach is logically and conceptually sound at an abstract level but of uncertain validity in its application to the empirical data.

Things get worse with their decision to deduct from the estimate of output loss a figure for the imputed value of leisure to the unemployed. What is in effect being assumed is that there is a voluntary element in *all* unemployment, which, given the fact that the voluntariness of any decision is a matter of degree, is perfectly reasonable. The problem is of course that voluntary unemployment *is* cost incurring because, being the unintended side-effect of the interaction of the tax and benefit systems, it is not voluntary from the societal perspective. Moreover, the value of leisure is not separately quantified but included in a single adjustment with black economy activity. So the treatment of leisure is flawed both in principle and in application. On balance, it may be concluded that the procedures followed by Okun (1962; 1970) and Junankar (1985) are more likely to yield an accurate estimate of the proportion of unemployment to be regarded as costless.

7.5 METHODS OF MEASURING THE OUTPUT LOSS OF COST-INCURRING UNEMPLOYMENT

Unemployment must be assumed to be cost incurring except when people who are officially classified as unemployed are frictionally unemployed, have permanently left or were never part of the labour force or are active in the black economy. The next problem is to measure the output loss from cost-incurring unemployment.

The most scrupulous method of doing this is based on the concept of the output gap and the method of measuring it that uses Okun's law (Okun, 1962; 1970). Its merits are best appreciated by reviewing other somewhat rudimentary approaches.

Perhaps the simplest approach to estimating the output loss caused by unemployment is to assume that everyone out of work would, if given a job, produce as much as the average person already in employment. If, for example, eliminating unemployment meant creating 10 per cent more jobs, then output would be 10 per cent higher and if that were to add, say, £30 billion to GDP, then unemployment would be costing the country £30 billion in lost output. Of course, in reality things are not so simple. The main problem is that the productivity of the unemployed is lower than average because they tend to be less skilled than the labour force as a whole. In 1975–81 unskilled men constituted only 6 per cent of the UK labour force but 40 per cent of the unemployed (Hughes and Hutchinson, 1986, p. 368). In the US unemployment in the early 1980s was four times as high among teenagers and three times as high among blacks as it was among white males aged 35–44 (Hughes and Perlman, 1984, Table 8.5, p. 192). These high incidence groups lacked experience or adequate training opportunities, or both. So it is likely that unemployed people have a lower productivity than the employed labour force. The average product method will therefore exaggerate the output loss caused by unemployment, unless of course the original estimate is corrected for the lower productivity of the unemployed.

The average wage approach assumes that the wages a worker is able to earn reflect the value of his or her output, so that output loss can be estimated by multiplying the number of unemployed people by average earnings. Obviously this method of measuring output loss is vulnerable to the same objections as the average product approach. Matthews and Minford use the average wage method adjusted for the lower productivity of the unemployed on the basis of evidence that the average previous earnings of the unemployed were 20 per cent below the national average (1987, p. 88). So far, so good. But they go on to make the adjustments for leisure and black economy activity which were either rejected outright or questioned in the previous section. The claim that the marginal value product of the unemployed *net of the value of their leisure and black economy output* is only about half of average national earnings is unlikely to be accurate.

The third method is to extrapolate the trend rate of output growth under full employment through the years of unemployment to estimate the potential rate of output growth during that time. If it is assumed that the recession of the early 1980s had never happened and that technological progress, investment and employment growth had continued at the rates seen in the 1960s and 1970s, it is in principle possible to extend the long-term trend rate of output growth into the 1980s. The difference between potential output estimated in this way and actual output is known as the output gap and affords a measure of the output loss associated with the rise in unemployment in the early 1980s. However, the gap between actual and potential output is greater than that indicated by a simple trend.

This is recognized in the Okun's law method of measuring output loss. The essential insight of this method is that a rise in officially recorded unemployment is only one symptom of the fact that the economy is operating below capacity. Accordingly, as economic activity recovers, 'a reduction in unemployment, measured as a percentage of the labor force, has a much larger than proportionate effect on output' (Okun, 1970, p. 140). As recorded unemployment falls, the participation rate and hence the size of the labour force increase; people who had given up looking for jobs come back into the labour force and some find work. If *all* the new jobs went to people who had previously been outside the labour force, the official unemployment rate would be unchanged but national output would be higher. Greater use is made of people already in employment through a rise in part-time work and overtime and a decline in hidden or 'on the job' unemployment. Clearly these factors must be taken into account in estimating the output gap, that is, the amount by which actual output falls short of potential output expressed as a percentage of potential output. The result reflects the full output loss incurred by running the economy below capacity. Estimating the output gap in this way is the most reliable method of measuring the output cost of unemployment.

7.6   EMPIRICAL ESTIMATES OF THE OUTPUT COSTS OF UNEMPLOYMENT

In the US Okun's method of calculating the output gap has been generally accepted in principle as the definitive procedure for measuring the output cost of unemployment. However, the original rate of output loss to unemployment of 3:1 was revised downwards for the second half of the 1970s to 2.25:1 (Gordon and Hall, 1980). But the output gap calculation applies only to unemployment in excess of the feasible full employment rate which had reached an estimated 6 per cent in the early 1980s. In other words, Okun's law or the output loss:unemployment ratio, is one element in the measurement of output loss as a percentage of GNP. Using Okun's law and assuming that six percentage points of recorded unemployment is costless yields reasonably convincing estimates of the output cost of US unemployment in the period 1980–83 (Table 7.2).

Table 7.2   US output loss estimates (% GNP) 1980–83

	Unemployment rate	GNP gap
1980	7.1	2.7
1981	7.5	3.2
1982	9.6	8.2
1983	9.4	6.7

Source: Dornbusch and Fischer (1987), frontispiece.

For the UK, the results of Junankar's (1985) investigation into the costs of unemployment in West Germany, France, Italy and the UK from 1980 to 1983 are more credible than the estimate made by Matthews and Minford (1987). Junankar's assumption about the proportion of official unemployment to be regarded as costless and accordingly excluded from the exercise appears to be closer to that implied by the threefold definition of costless unemployment, except for the failure to take account of black economy output. All four methods of measuring the output loss associated with cost-incurring unemployment were used in this investigation. Since the Okun's law method appears to be the most reliable approach (when used with the 1974–79 full employment baseline) the output cost of unemployment in 1983, for example, can be said with some confidence to be almost 14 per cent of GDP (column 4, Table 7.3). But in view of the theoretical and practical problems which beset the measurement of output loss through unemployment, it is no surprise to see that Junankar averages the results of the four methods (column 5, Table 7.3). Even so, the result is an output cost in 1983 of about 11–12 per cent of GDP a year.

Table 7.3   UK output loss estimates (% GDP) 1980–83

	Average product	Average wage	Trend	Okun	Average
1980	2.1– 3.6	2.1– 3.7	6.8	3.0– 6.5	3.5– 5.2
1981	5.8– 7.4	6.5– 8.3	10.6	9.5–13.1	8.1– 9.8
1982	7.5– 9.1	8.7–10.6	11.1	12.3–15.8	9.9–11.7
1983	8.5–10.0	9.9–11.8	10.8	13.7–17.2	10.7–12.5

Note: All but Trend results include low and high estimates of output loss. Except when using the Trend method, measuring output loss involves comparing output during unemployment with output under full employment. Unemployment in the 1980s is measured against unemployment during the two previous periods, 1968–73 and 1974–79, that is, against feasible approximations to full employment. Three of the methods produce broadly similar estimates of output loss; as expected, the Okun results are consistently higher than the others. The fifth column averages the results shown in the first four and is therefore a compromise estimate.

Source: Junankar (1985), Table 4.13, p. 41.

The cumulative effect of output loss on the scale seen in the recession of the early 1980s is dramatic: 'at 1982 levels of unemployment, the equivalent of a whole year's GNP would be lost in less than a decade in both the US and the UK' (Hughes and Perlman, 1984, p. 217).

7.7   CONCLUSION

There is deep disagreement among economists about the output costs of unemployment. Estimates of the output loss incurred by unemployment at the level seen in the UK at the end of the recession of the early 1980s vary from 2 per cent to 13–17 per cent of GDP. Two sources of disagreement have been identified.

First there is the dispute over the extent to which the official unemployment figures include people who are voluntarily out of work, the assumption being that only involuntary unemployment incurs output loss. I have challenged that assumption and argued that the distinction between voluntary and involuntary unemployment is not the same as that between costless and cost-incurring unemployment. Since the rate of cost-incurring UK unemployment in the early 1980s turns out to be close to the official unemployment rate, this approach vindicates the higher estimates of the output costs of unemployment. The result is less decisive in the US, where the official unemployment figures for the same period included six percentage points of costless unemployment.

Second, there is the question of how to measure the output loss associated with cost-incurring unemployment. A review of the principal methods left little doubt that the Okun's law approach is likely to be the most accurate. Again, this outcome favours the higher estimates of the output costs of unemployment.

For the UK an unemployment rate of almost 11 per cent in 1983 entailed the loss of at least 11–12 per cent and probably 14 per cent of potential GDP. In the US, an unemployment rate of 9 per cent was associated with the loss of almost 7 per cent of GNP. It seems then that the unemployment rate:output loss ratio is unlikely to be very far from 1:1, marginally higher for the UK and slightly lower for the US.

8. The Redistributive Effects of Unemployment

8.1 WHY LOSING OUTPUT MATTERS

The real cost of unemployment is the loss of potential output, which at 1983 levels of unemployment probably amounted to a little less than 10 per cent of GNP in the US and a little more than 10 per cent of GDP in the UK. This is the only real material or financial loss involved in unemployment. The extra money the government must raise to pay unemployment benefits and make good the loss of income tax revenues from people who have lost their jobs is not an additional cost of unemployment. What is happening here is not that the economy is losing even more output but rather that the government is transferring some income from taxpayers to the unemployed. The question is to what extent this transfer protects the unemployed from suffering the full effects of the lost output themselves. Answering this question does *not* involve calculating a pecuniary magnitude to be added to the estimates of output loss in order to find the 'total' costs of unemployment.

What it is essential to understand is that there are two different questions to be asked about one and the same phenomenon, the loss of potential output through unemployment. The first is simply 'How much output was lost?' It is a simple and obvious question to ask but if the previous chapter did nothing else it probably made it clear that there is no simple and obvious answer. Still, it is possible to put a figure on the output cost of unemployment with a reasonable degree of confidence. The problem is that someone might react to being told that 10 per cent of a year's potential output has been lost by saying 'So what? Does it really make any difference to anyone? Isn't this just another manifestation of the economist's professional obsession with maximizing everything?' To put it more formally, the second question about the output cost of unemployment is: 'What difference does the loss of potential output make to people's well-being?' The aim of this chapter is to offer part of the answer to that question.

The 'So what?' response illustrates the rather intangible nature of the concept of lost potential output. The loss of goods that might have been manufactured but were not and never will be may appear a somewhat abstract or hypothetical deprivation. Yet this loss of potential output does have serious effects on people's well-being. People's incomes are lower than they otherwise would be, either because they have lost their jobs or because they are paying higher taxes. In principle, everyone in the labour force bears some of the output cost of unemployment, the unemployed by being only partly compensated for their loss of earnings and taxpayers by experiencing a fall in after-tax income as taxes are increased to finance the payment of benefits to the unemployed. So the burden or incidence of the loss of output associated with unemployment depends on the extent to which welfare benefits compensate the unemployed for their loss of earned income.

In this chapter an attempt is made to assess the impact of unemployment on the distribution of income by examining the monetary loss to the unemployed and the fiscal or Exchequer cost to the government and ultimately to taxpayers. It will be argued that in both the US and the UK unemployment imposes a severe financial penalty on most unemployed people. A large part of the incidence of the output loss associated with unemployment falls on the unemployed. Not all of it, it is true, but unemployment nevertheless involves a net transfer of income from what is already the least generously rewarded section of the labour force.

8.2   THE FINANCIAL IMPACT OF UNEMPLOYMENT ON THE UNEMPLOYED

The central concept used in estimating the financial impact of unemployment on the unemployed is the replacement ratio, which measures the extent to which the loss of earnings caused by being unemployed is made good by benefits. In calculating the replacement ratio as a measure of the loss of income contingent upon becoming unemployed, net income from benefits while unemployed is expressed as a percentage of net income when last in full-time work. So an assumption has to be made about the level of previous earnings. But assumptions also have to be made about the duration of unemployment, marital status, the number of children in the family and so on, because these things influence the level of unemployment benefits.

The average replacement ratio is a commonly used but not terribly informative measure of the monetary cost of unemployment to the unemployed. A weighted average of replacement ratios for different family types is calculated, the weights reflecting the percentage of unemployed people belonging to each family type. For example, married couples with four or more children have the highest replacement ratio but comprise only a small fraction of the unemployed. In the UK, this average replacement ratio rose substantially in the late 1950s and early 1960s (Figure 8.1). A further sharp increase took place during the Thatcher government's first term (1979–83). The average replacement ratio

Figure 8.1   Average UK replacement ratio 1950–85

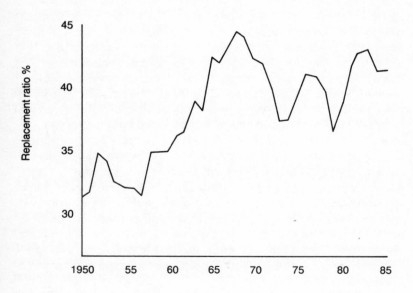

Source: Layard (1986), Figure 16, p. 49.

had fallen a little by 1985, when it was still slightly higher than it was in the middle 1970s under Labour.

The average replacement ratio is not very informative about the replacement ratios actually faced by unemployed people and hence about the actual financial losses incurred by different households through unemployment. The problem is that this ratio is calculated on the basis of male manual average earnings. But the unemployed are less skilled and less qualified than the labour force as a whole, so they earned below-average incomes when last in work and expect below-average earnings on returning to employment. It is more illuminating to examine replacement ratios for selected family types at different levels of gross income while in work and when unemployed. The lower the replacement ratio, the greater the financial penalty incurred through unemployment. Conversely, the higher the replacement ratio, the greater the risk of a disincentive effect. In the extreme, the unemployment trap occurs when net income from social security benefits while unemployed is greater than net income when last in full-time work, so that the replacement ratio is greater than 100 per cent.

It is clear that in the UK most unemployed people face serious financial hardship on losing their jobs and that the unemployment trap applies only to a small minority (Figure 8.2). Of the four family types illustrated, the replacement ratio was greater than 100 per cent, so that the jobless person was actually 'better off on the dole', only for married couples with four or more children, previously earning as little as £50–£70 per week (£2 600–£3 640 per annum). The situation was only marginally different for married couples with two children, who faced a replacement ratio of 90 per cent at the same very low level of former gross earnings. Replacement ratios remained high for two family types right up to average male manual earnings (£180 per week). Married men with four or more children (comprising only 3 per cent of male unemployed) had a replacement ratio which did not fall below 90 per cent until former gross earnings of £170 per week. Likewise, married men with two children, accounting for 10 per cent of male unemployed, had a replacement ratio of at least 85 per cent up to £140 per week, or roughly three-quarters of average male manual earnings.

On the other hand, two groups which together constitute 70 per cent of male unemployment faced substantially lower replacement ratios. Married men with no children, comprising 20 per cent of male unemployment, found their replacement ratio falling sharply as former gross earnings rose, from 86 per cent at earnings of £90 per week (half of the average male manual earnings) to 58 per cent at £180 per week. Single men account for 50 per cent of male unemployed and, assuming that they are childless, faced a replacement ratio of 68 per cent at £90 per week, falling to less than 40 per cent at £180 per week. A weighted average of these four replacement ratios is greater than 80 per cent only for former gross earnings of up to £100 per week and then declines sharply to 53 per cent at £180 per week. During the period 1973 to 1981 between 21 per cent and 30 per cent of people under pension age who were eligible for supplementary benefit did not in fact claim it (Atkinson, 1985, p. 80). The reasons for incomplete take-up include the complexity of claims procedures and the deterrent effect on genuine claimants of administrative efforts to investigate fraud. In the light of all these facts, it is clear that in the UK unemployment entails a major loss of income for the majority of households and indeed a financial catastrophe for many of them.

Detailed evidence on the monetary cost of unemployment to the unemployed in the US is harder to obtain, not least because the eligibility conditions for unemployment benefits vary from state to state. Feldstein (1974) saw unemployment compensation as a tax on the income an unemployed person would earn if re-employed and accordingly calculated a net tax rate, defined as the ratio of unemployment benefits to prospective net (or after-tax) earnings. This net tax rate is a version of the replacement ratio but one intended to measure the possible disincentive effect of unemployment benefits rather than the financial penalty of unemployment. That is why unemployment benefits are expressed as a percentage of *prospective* rather than previous earnings. However, prospective earnings are obviously a matter of guesswork and there is no alternative but to use earnings when last in work as a proxy. Consequently, Feldstein's net tax rate doubles as a measure of the monetary cost of unemployment as well as the disincentive effect of unemployment compensation. For single men, the net tax rate varied across states from 40 per cent to 84 per cent with an average of 63 per cent. The average figure for a married man on median male earnings was 60 per cent, rising to

Figure 8.2   Replacement ratios by family type and former gross earnings

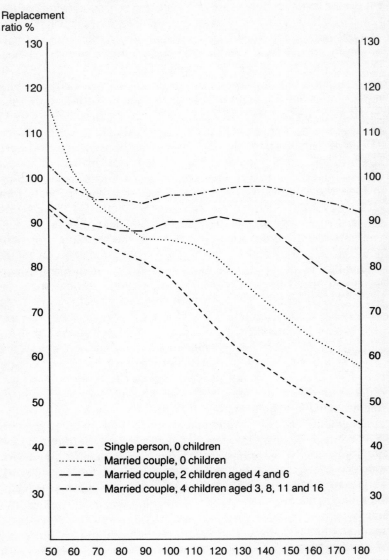

Replacement
ratio %

Single person, 0 children
Married couple, 0 children
Married couple, 2 children aged 4 and 6
Married couple, 4 children aged 3, 8, 11 and 16

Former gross earnings £ per week

Notes to Figure 8.2: The replacement ratios were calculated by expressing net available income when in work as a percentage of net available income while unemployed. In April 1987, net available income or total income support (TIS) was calculated according to the following formula: earnings + social security benefits + housing benefit + free school meals + welfare milk − (income tax + national insurance contributions + rent and rates + fares to work).

Supplementary benefit (SB) was the major source of income for the unemployed. In February 1986, when 3.3 million people were unemployed, 2.1 million of them were receiving SB, most of whom (1.7 million) were relying on SB without unemployment benefit (UB). Under the pre-1988 system, SB was paid if *net* family income fell below a certain level. SB was therefore paid to (1) everybody after 12 months of unemployment, when UB ceased, (2) those disqualified from UB for any of the four reasons given below, (3) to some UB claimants in addition to UB and (4) to people in low-income full-time work. Once receiving SB, a person was also entitled to 'passported benefits', e.g., free school meals and housing benefit (HB), which consisted of rent and rates rebates calculated on the basis of *gross* income. The amount of SB depended on marital status and on the number of children in the family, something which was not true of UB.

UB was paid for the first 12 months of unemployment, provided a person was (1) available for work and (2) had adequate national insurance contributions. However, delays sometimes occurred while a claimant's entitlement to UB was determined and UB was not paid for the first 13 weeks of unemployment if the claimant had left his/her last job for no good reason.

The situation was more complicated for unemployed people whose entitlement to family income supplement (FIS), for which they qualified because their *gross* income when last in work was below a certain level, was still current. The total benefits available to single parents and married couples with children varied according to their former gross income.

In April 1988 the social security benefit system was reformed with the intention of improving the targeting of benefits on groups regarded as most in need of financial help.

Source: Department of Health and Social Security, *Tax/Benefit Model Tables*, November 1987.

69 per cent for a married man on approximately two-thirds of median male earnings.

The picture is not radically altered by two more up-to-date estimates of the financial cost of unemployment to unemployed people. Dornbusch and Fischer (1987) quote figures for 1983 which compare median family incomes during unemployment and while one family member is employed. Unemployment benefits for a married man amounted to 66 per cent of normal income from employment. Baumol and Blinder (1988) found the average unemployment benefit in 1986 to be $136 per week or 45 per cent of average earnings. Clearly, unemployment in the US is likely to entail a sharp drop in income, at least for married couples close to average earnings.

8.3   THE FISCAL COST OF UNEMPLOYMENT

The monetary cost of unemployment to unemployed people represents part of the incidence of the lost potential output, which is the only real cost of unemployment so far identified. The rest of the incidence of output loss is accounted for by the fiscal or Exchequer cost of unemployment, which measures the impact of unemployment on the public finances. An increase in unemployment affects the government's budget in two ways: by reducing the inflow of income tax revenues as people lose their jobs, and by raising the amount of money that has to be paid out to unemployment benefit claimants. This appears to be simple enough in principle but a number of disputes have arisen over how the fiscal cost of unemployment should be understood and measured in practice.

In the first place, it is not unanimously agreed that the fiscal cost of unemployment is part of the incidence of output loss and hence not in itself a real or an additional cost. Proctor (1987), for example, puts the fiscal cost of UK unemployment in 1986 at £15 billion and adds that sum to an estimated output loss of £40 billion: the 'total cost therefore if we include all of these items is £55bn., approximately' (1987, p. 11). This procedure clearly involves double-counting, because it overlooks the fact that national output and national income are simply two alternative ways of measuring one and the same series of economic activities. It has already been argued that the loss of output is a failure to realize potential; goods that might have been made will not be made and income that might have been earned will not be earned. Lost output means lost income; under unemployment incomes are lower than they otherwise would be. The incomes of those people unlucky enough to have lost their jobs are substantially lower than they would have been from continued employment. The net incomes of those people fortunate enough to remain in employment are reduced by the need to pay higher taxes. So the fiscal cost of unemployment is not an additional loss but part of the incidence of output loss.

In measuring the fiscal cost of unemployment, the main problem is where to draw the line in tracing the fiscal implications of a rise in unemployment. There is no disagreement about including income tax and, for the UK, national insurance contributions lost to the Exchequer when people lose their jobs. Neither is there a problem about adding the money paid out to those people when they claim unemployment benefit, with the associated administrative expenses. But what about indirect or expenditure taxes? The Treasury (1981) estimated only the direct or first-round Exchequer costs of an increase of 100 000 in registered unemployment and therefore omitted expenditure taxes. However, when people become unemployed, they typically experience a significant or even catastrophic fall in disposable income and so must be presumed to curtail their consumer spending. Accordingly, in measuring the fiscal cost of unemployment Junankar (1985) goes further than the Treasury and includes an estimate of the associated loss of expenditure taxes.

The other question that arises in calculating the direct Exchequer costs of unemployment is whether to include government expenditure on special employment measures. Hughes and Perlman (1984, p. 215) dismiss the claim that this expenditure is an additional fiscal cost on the grounds that in so far as such measures are successful they reduce unemployment and lead to savings elsewhere, presumably on unemployment benefits. Against this it might be argued that job creation schemes and labour subsidies do not provide 'real' jobs but are merely a disguised form of unemployment. The decisive question is whether there is a return on such expenditure in the form of output. If there is not, it is a transfer payment and therefore just as much a cost to the Exchequer as unemployment benefits. However, it seems reasonably clear that there *is* a return on special employment measures. Even if the market value of the goods produced by the participants on such schemes is less than the cost of employing them, output in the future will be higher than it otherwise would have been because valuable skills and attitudes will have been preserved. This consideration vindicates most estimates of UK fiscal costs (for example H.M. Treasury, 1981; Dilnot and Morris, 1981; Junankar, 1985), which exclude expenditure on special employment measures.

The studies by Dilnot and Morris (undated) and Junankar (1985) succeed in gauging the order of magnitude of the more immediate fiscal costs of unemployment in the UK. The usefulness of the estimate made by H.M. Treasury (1981) is limited. The direct Exchequer cost (excluding expenditure taxes) of an increase of 100 000 in registered unemployment from the 1980–81 level of a little more than 2 million was found to be £340 million. But this figure cannot be generalized to arrive at an estimate of the direct Exchequer cost of total unemployment. The reason is that assumptions had to be made about (a) the family characteristics of the 100 000 newly unemployed people in order to assess their benefit entitlements and (b) their earnings had they remained in work, in order to estimate the income tax and national insurance contributions they would have paid. It was felt that it would be unsafe to believe that these assumptions were true of all of the 2 million people who were already out of work. That leaves the two later studies (Table 8.1). Their findings are strikingly similar until 1982–83 and even then the divergence, in which the largest single factor is a difference in the estimates of lost expenditure taxes, is not enough to destroy confidence in them as guides to the order of magnitude of the fiscal costs of unemployment in the UK.

Table 8.1   The fiscal cost of unemployment: UK 1979–80 to
*   1983–84*

£ millions at current prices

	1979–80	1980–81	1981–82	1982–83	1983–84
Total Exchequer cost					
Junankar	4 447	7 804	12 800	16 268	16 768
Dilnot and Morris	4 423	7 807	12 947	13 707	13 567
% GDP					
Junankar	2.17	3.30	4.92	5.74	5.49
Dilnot and Morris	2.07	3.30	4.98	4.84	4.44

Source: Junankar (1985), Table 5.6, p. 57.

These estimates of the Exchequer costs of unemployment appear to be reliable as far as they go but they do not attempt to measure the longer-term effects of unemployment on the public purse. Such an exercise would encounter enormous difficulties, caused mainly by uncertainty about how the government would choose to finance the 'fiscal gap' which opens up when benefit expenditure rises and tax receipts fall. It has been assumed so far that taxpayers meet the fiscal costs of unemployment by paying higher taxes. This is a convenient way of expressing the fact that fiscal costs represent part of the incidence of output loss, specifically the part met by society as a whole rather than the unemployed in particular. But of course the government does not *have* to close the fiscal gap by increasing taxes by the full amount. It could instead transfer money from other spending programmes, in which case the incidence would fall not on taxpayers but on the would-be recipients of the services that were cut back. The other alternative is borrowing, which shifts the incidence on to future taxpayers, although interest rates might rise, with implications for mortgage holders and borrowers. In Keynesian demand management theory, the borrowing option turns the Exchequer costs of unemployment into automatic stabilizers offsetting the fall in aggregate demand that caused the unemployment in the first place. So borrowing, or deficit finance, to cover the short-term fiscal costs is a means of reducing the overall output loss involved in unemployment. In certain circumstances it is even possible that the deferred fiscal costs can be met from a higher rate of growth than would have been achieved without deficit finance, in which case there is no net cost at all. These intriguing implications of financing the fiscal costs of unemployment are beyond the scope of the studies examined in this section.

Once again, information about the fiscal costs of unemployment in the US is limited. The Congressional Budget Office is reported as estimating in 1980 that each 1 percentage point rise in the unemployment rate increases the federal budget deficit by approximately $25 billion (Hughes and Perlman, 1984, p. 215). This general claim is vulnerable to the objection that it depends on the previous earnings and family circumstances of newly unemployed people remaining constant each time the unemployment rate rises by 1 percentage point. Subject to this qualification, the fiscal cost of total US unemployment in 1980 was perhaps in the order of $180 billion, or 6.58 per cent of GNP.

8.4 CONCLUSION: THE MATERIAL BURDEN OF OUTPUT LOSS

What conclusion about the redistributive effects of unemployment is implied by the evidence examined in this chapter? The most important point to have emerged is that unemployment affects the distribution of income by inflicting the incidence of output loss disproportionately on the unemployed. This is clear from two pieces of evidence, which probably deserve the title 'facts'. The first is that unemployment is a major financial crisis for the majority of unemployed people. A replacement ratio as high as 80 per cent still entails a loss of no less than one-fifth of previous income. It is hard to think of any other circumstances in which a household loses one-fifth of its accustomed income 'at a stroke'. Moreover, most people in work in the UK and the US look forward to, and come to take for granted, steadily rising real incomes year by year. Suppose the government announced a pay freeze at a time when prices were rising at 5 per cent a year. It can hardly be expected that people would be indifferent to a prospective 5 per cent drop in real income. Such a policy would be announced with all the rhetoric of hard slog, belt-tightening and sacrifice today for prosperity tomorrow. A 5 per cent fall in real income is no small thing. For many people, unemployment means a much greater drop.

Worse, the people who experience unemployment and the financial hardship associated with it are typically in jobs paying below-average wages. So the incidence of the output cost of unemployment falls most heavily on the poorer sections of society. A few figures are enough to indicate the scale of the regressive redistribution of income that unemployment entails. For the UK, the total Exchequer cost of unemployment in 1983–84 was approximately 5 per cent, averaging the estimates of Junankar (1985) and Dilnot and Morris (1981) (Table 8.1). The most credible estimate of output loss in 1983 came to almost 14 per cent of GDP (see Table 7.3). So almost two-thirds of the incidence of that output loss fell upon the 10.8 per cent of the labour force that was unemployed. This implies that the financial impact of unemployment on the average unemployed person was about 18 times greater than it was on the average working and taxpaying member of the labour force. It is surely clear beyond reasonable doubt that unemployment has a severe financial impact on the unemployed and a regressive effect on the distribution of income.

9. The Human Costs of Unemployment

9.1 THE SIGNIFICANCE OF THE HUMAN COSTS OF UNEMPLOYMENT

This is to be the last chapter on the costs of unemployment and it will also be the shortest. Are the human costs of unemployment a less serious matter than the output costs and their incidence? Not necessarily; the position and brevity of this chapter reflects the lack of hard facts about some of the human costs of unemployment and the limitations of the standard methods of the human sciences as a means of investigating the others. For all we know, the human costs of unemployment are the ones that matter most but we do not know enough about them to be sure. The first question is: What precisely is meant by the term 'the human costs of unemployment'?

The basic intention in using this term is to identify the further effects of unemployment on the well-being of people over and above the financial impact of unemployment on unemployed individuals and taxpayers. How are people's lives affected by the major loss of income normally contingent upon becoming unemployed? Apart from income, what else do people lose when they lose their jobs? Is anyone else affected, for example people living in areas of high unemployment? The idea of the human costs is, then, to focus on the non-pecuniary effects of unemployment.

Three distinct effects are covered by this general concept. First, there is some empirical evidence that unemployment leads to a deterioration in mental health. Certainly at least some unemployed people, and their families, experience anxiety and despair, frustration and desperate unhappiness. Second, on physical health, some studies have found a statistical association between unemployment and mortality or a specific cause of death. Perhaps the psychological pressure of unemployment causes some people to suffer stress-related illnesses. Third, there are the costs of unemployment, apart from output loss, which are imposed on people other than the unemployed themselves and their families, principally the alleged rise in unemployment-related crime. The suggestion here is that people who are not themselves unemployed but who live in an area of high unemployment become the victims of crimes committed by unemployed people.

The significance of these adverse effects on human well-being is that they represent extra costs of unemployment which it would in principle make sense to add to the loss of potential output in order to determine the aggregate costs of unemployment. The loss of potential output can be thought of as the material cost of unemployment in that its real effect is to reduce the material standard of living of the unemployed and, although to a much lesser extent, of taxpayers. The main focus of economics is on the allocation of scarce resources to the production of goods which satisfy human wants or, in other words, on the material standard of living. Of course, human well-being is a wider concept than the material standard of living, encompassing everything that contributes to people's health and happiness. Mental or psychological health, physical health and the quality of life are the three aspects of this wider concept of human well-being that are captured by the idea of the human costs of unemployment.

9.2   THE PSYCHOLOGICAL IMPACT OF UNEMPLOYMENT

Unemployment might be expected to have an adverse effect on the psychological well-being of unemployed people and their families. Those who suffer a substantial loss of income are likely to experience stress and conflict as they struggle to pay their bills and maintain an acceptable standard of living. Losing a job often means losing the friendships and, perhaps even more damagingly, the sense of identity and the self-esteem that went with it. But there is no denying that some unemployed people appear to be relatively untroubled by their situation and others actually prefer to be jobless. On the face of it, the question seems to be how many unemployed people there are in each category.

In reality it is not as simple as that. The subjective experience of unemployment can be either demoralizing or liberating. What frees one person from boredom, subservience or toil can leave another bereft of opportunities to exercise valued skills, construct a social life and pursue ambitions. Even if unemployment always came as a harsh blow reactions to it would vary, for the adversity that crushes one individual spurs another to renewed efforts in a different direction. Again, if a majority of unemployed people are able to get a lot out of life, that does not mean that unemployment is merely an irritant. It may indicate the moral strength invested in coming to terms with a catastrophe. Consequently, the mental health of an unemployed person reflects that person's response to his or her situation as well as the situation itself, so it is not an objective measure of the psychological impact of unemployment.

Still, some attempt must be made to estimate the degree and extent of the psychological damage. There are three complications in such a project. First, instead of a simple dichotomy between those who are desperate for work and those who are reasonably content to stay on the dole, there is a continuum from those who are driven to mental collapse and even suicide through those who tolerate their situation while striving with varying degrees of effort to get out of it to those whose endeavours are directed towards avoiding job offers. Second, it is unlikely that the long-term unemployed will feel the same way about their unemployment after a year as they did on the day it began. Some people will occupy different positions along the continuum at different times. Third, there is the possibility that psychological problems such as anxiety or depression are part of the explanation of an individual's unemployment rather than some of its effects.

Longitudinal studies by psychologists using standardized interview schedules have done much to overcome these difficulties. A longitudinal investigation follows people over a period of time during which they move into and out of unemployment. This makes it possible to identify people who experience psychological problems in work which might be contributory factors in causing them to become unemployed. It also enables the investigator to record changes in the psychological state of people who undergo a long period of unemployment. So longitudinal studies hold out the prospect of resolving the second and third complications. The use of standardized interview schedules is a response to the first. The problem here is to try to combine the best features of two very different investigatory techniques. At one end of the scale, an interviewer might do no more than prompt unemployed people to speak for themselves, eschewing formal questions which risk putting words into the mouths of those being interviewed. The result can at best be no more than an in-depth insider's understanding of what it is like to be unemployed *for the inevitably small sample of unemployed people interviewed*. At the other extreme, questionnaires can provide quantifiable information about relatively large numbers of unemployed people but only at a rather superficial level.

The basic insight underlying longitudinal studies of the psychological effects of unemployment is that jobs perform valuable 'latent functions'. This simply means that jobs provide satisfactions over and above the monetary rewards that people might offer as their reason for working. Jobs impose a time structure on the day, provide contact with other people, confer status and identity and show that there are goals and purposes beyond the scope of the individual (see Jahoda, 1982). The loss of these latent functions constitutes the psychological damage done by unemployment. Expanding this list of latent functions, Warr (1987) identifies nine factors affecting the level of mental health both in work and during unemployment. These are self-explanatory, except for 'environmental clarity', which refers to the degree to which there is an expected and appropriate way of behaving in a particular social environment. The general idea is that when a person becomes unemployed, he or she moves into an environment where each of the nine characteristics is less favourable to mental health (Figure 9.1). The overlap represents working environments ('dead-end' jobs, for example) which are no better for mental health than unemployment.

The principal conclusion about unemployment and mental health reached by Warr is that 'longitudinal research has demonstrated a substantial negative impact upon several aspects of mental health: people visibly deteriorate across time' (ibid., p. 2). An index of mental ill-health based on the categories in Figure 9.1 has a mean value for unemployed men of 35 against 19 for employed men. Middle-aged men (40–49 years) appear to be most seriously harmed by unemployment, scoring 38 on the mental ill-health index, because financial pressures are compounded by the loss of valued social roles as member of a work group and

Figure 9.1   Employment, unemployment and mental health

← Low	Mental health	→ High
←	Opportunity for control	→
←	Opportunity for skill use	→
←	Externally generated goals	→
←	Variety	→
←	Environmental clarity	→
←	Availability of money	→
←	Physical security	→
←	Interpersonal contact	→
←	Valued social position	→
UNEMPLOYMENT		EMPLOYMENT

Source: Warr (1987).

breadwinner for the family. What these figures indicate is that unemployment is associated with symptoms such as 'feelings of strain, sleep loss through worry, lack of confidence, inability to concentrate, feelings of depression, irritation and anxiety, a sense of personal worthlessness and so on' (ibid.). A typical pattern is a rapid decline in mental health during the first six months of unemployment, followed by stabilization as people become resigned to their situation. There is a similarity here to the sequence of stages illustrated in Figure 9.2.

It seems to be beyond any reasonable doubt that unemployment inflicts anxiety and frustration on almost all unemployed people at some stage and imposes anguish and despair on a minority who are not equipped to cope with extreme misfortune. Economics does not possess a calculus to evaluate the desperate suffering of a few against tolerable worries spread among many. Listening to the unemployed makes it plain that doing justice to the psychological costs of unemployment involves trying to appreciate the intensity of the mental turmoil experienced by some individuals. Dawson (1988) reports the following comments made by people soon after they became unemployed: 'I received ten minutes notice in being made redundant.' At the start unemployment can feel like liberation: 'I felt better – money in the bank – less tired

Figure 9.2   The experience of unemployment

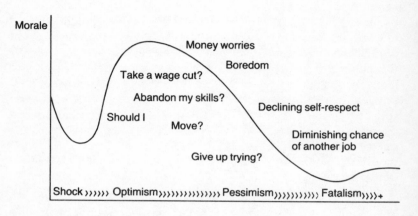

Source: Junankar (1985), Diagram 6.1, p. 66.

– plenty of fresh air – an opportunity to do other things with my life without the frustrations and claustrophobia of factory life.' A couple of years on it was a different story: 'depressed and insecure, no success in finding even part-time work to supplement savings'. There is desperation among other long-term unemployed men: 'Yes, whenever I get a sufficient amount or come into money I spend it fast, mostly on drink. I seem to panic when I have money to spend.' 'To survive this unwanted gap in one's life one has to be either half-drunk or half-crazy most of the time it seems.' 'I feel like an autistic child in relation to other working folk.'

9.3 THE EFFECT OF UNEMPLOYMENT ON PHYSICAL HEALTH

The measurement of the effect of unemployment on physical health faces somewhat similar problems to the investigation of its psychological impact. The unemployed are less healthy than those in work, but can we be sure that their ill-health is the consequence of their unemployment? Perhaps it is the less healthy members of the labour force who are most likely to be 'selected' for unemployment. Unfortunately, research into the effect of unemployment on physical health is dominated, not by longitudinal studies of the sort that proved so useful in isolating its psychological consequences, but by statistical analysis. This attempts to answer the question: Is there a statistical link between changes in unemployment and changes in physical health? If there is, there is a question of interpretation: Does this statistical association indicate a causal connection? Does it mean that unemployment is a *cause* of ill-health?

To answer the first question changes in some indicator of the health of the population, such as the mortality rate, are compared with changes in the factors that might influence it, such as diet, medical progress and of course unemployment. Suppose that only one of these factors, say unemployment, rose whenever the mortality rate rose and fell whenever the mortality rate fell. Then the answer to the first question would be: yes, changes in the rate of unemployment are correlated with changes in the mortality rate. In other words, whenever there is an increase in the number of people out of work there is also an increase in the number of deaths per thousand of the population. An American sociologist, J. Harvey Brenner, has found unemployment to be significantly correlated with mortality and with some specific causes of death. The results for the US are shown in Table 9.1. For the UK over the period 1936–76, Brenner (1979) used mortality rates for different age groups and found that unemployment was significantly correlated with mortality at all ages.

There are convincing grounds for scepticism about these results. Other researchers using similar data and statistical techniques have failed to confirm Brenner's findings. Gravelle, Hutchinson and Stern (1981), for example, found that the significant correlation between unemployment and mortality disappeared when the

Table 9.1   Unemployment and physical health: US 1970

	Increase resulting from 1% higher unemployment over six-year period
Total mortality	36 890
Cardiovascular mortality	20 240
Suicide	920
Cirrhosis of liver mortality	495

Source: Brenner (1977).

time period was extended to 1922–76 or divided into two at 1951. The reason is that the shorter time period gives undue weight to a single and very large fall in unemployment in the early 1940s, from almost 10 per cent in 1940 to less than 1 per cent in 1942, which occurred while mortality was also falling rapidly. If that one episode is put into a longer perspective, or taken out altogether by looking at the period 1951–76, unemployment is no longer found to be correlated with mortality. Moreover, there is another possible explanation of the fall in mortality in the early 1940s. Perhaps surprisingly, diet improved during the years of the Second World War, especially among low-income groups (Greaves and Hollingsworth, 1966). Was it the fall in unemployment which led to reduced mortality or was it the improvement in diet? Since the two competing explanatory variables, unemployment and diet, moved in the same direction at the same time, it is impossible to find a unique correlation between either one of them and mortality.

Even if unemployment *is* correlated with mortality and with some specific causes of death, this does not necessarily mean that unemployment is a *cause* of ill-health and death. The reason lies in the philosophical problem of induction: no matter how many times event A has been observed to be followed by event B, it is always possible that the next time A is seen it will *not* be followed by B. There is always a first time. The fact that in the past the sun has risen every morning is no logical guarantee that it will ever do so again. However, the idea that A is the cause of B is usually taken to imply that if A happens then B must happen too. So observing that A has so far always been followed by B does not entail that A is the cause of B. Still less does the fact that events of type A are significantly correlated with events of type B, that A-events are on many *but not all* occasions followed by B-events, entail that events of type A cause events of type B. The correlation could be a misleading or spurious one. Hendry (1980), for example, found that cumulated annual rainfall was just as closely correlated with the inflation rate as was the money supply.

So it is always possible that even if a correlation were to be established between unemployment and mortality, it would be spurious. In the first place, there might be some unknown factor which is causally responsible for the movements in *both* unemployment and physical health indicators. A second point is that the causal connection might be the other way round, differences in the health status of working people explaining in part why certain individuals and not others are the ones who lose their jobs when unemployment rises. For example, their poor health may have prevented them from gaining the qualifications necessary to take them out of the unskilled jobs which were most vulnerable in the recession of the early 1980s. Finally, economic theory suggests that *reported* ill-health will increase in line with unemployment even if the actual health status of the population is unchanged. The reason is simply that the opportunity cost of visiting a doctor is much lower for unemployed people, who stand to lose only their leisure rather than wages for time off work.

Changes in unemployment are not correlated with variations in mortality and even if they were the correlation would be open to several conflicting interpretations. In the absence of reliable longitudinal studies of the physical health of people as they move in and out of unemployment, there is no compelling reason to believe that unemployment has a significant adverse effect on the physical health of the unemployed.

9.4 THE EXTERNAL COSTS OF UNEMPLOYMENT

The external costs of unemployment are its effects on people other than the unemployed and their families. Research has concentrated on the alleged link between unemployment and crime. The suggestion is that unemployment leads people who would not otherwise become involved in criminal activity to commit crimes. Perhaps they simply have more time, perhaps they are under financial pressure or perhaps they act out of frustration and resentment. The external costs of unemployment would be reckoned in terms of the injuries or material losses suffered by their victims and the monetary cost to the authorities of investigating these crimes.

Most investigations of the claim that unemployment leads to an increase in criminal activity look for correlations between changes in the unemployment rate and changes in recorded crime rates. There is no shortage of studies reporting a positive correlation (Freeman, 1983). However, there are two reasons for rejecting this statistical association as evidence for the hypothesis that unemployment leads to crime. First, *anything* that has increased substantially over the last 30 years is almost bound to be correlated with the officially recorded crime rate. Tarling (1982) cites the consumption of ice cream. This is pure coincidence, so perhaps the correlation between unemployment and recorded crime is too. Second, part of the apparent increase in the crime rate is illusory. Carr-Hill and Stern argue that a 'major part, possibly most, of the increase in recorded crime may be due to the increase in the proportion of offences recorded rather than in the number of offences which occur' (1983, p. 391). The extent of any increase in the number of actual offences is simply not known.

9.5 CONCLUSION

There is little doubt that the human costs of unemployment are substantial. Unemployed people and their families tend to experience a deterioration in their psychological well-being, ranging from anxiety and boredom to severe depression and despair. There is a greater incidence of physical ill-health among the unemployed but the extent to which this reflects a prior record of poor physical health is not clear. No causal connection between unemployment and crime has been established to support the claim that unemployment imposes significant external costs on society. So it is the psychological impact of unemployment on unemployed people and their families that is known to account for the human costs of unemployment.

10. The Redistributive Effects of Moderate Unanticipated Inflation

10.1 THE MAINSTREAM DEBATE ON THE REDISTRIBUTIVE EFFECTS OF INFLATION

Inflation, in so far as it is not anticipated, changes the distribution of income and wealth. If a correct inflation forecast were incorporated into every decision made by economic agents, the costs and benefits of one activity would be unchanged relative to those of another. There would be no reason to switch from one economic activity to another. In reality of course inflation is never perfectly anticipated. People who are fortunate or clever enough to find that their money incomes increase by at least as much as inflation gain in purchasing power in comparison with those whose money incomes fail to rise in step with inflation. So inflation redistributes income in various directions, depending on the speed with which different social groups react to it. The redistributive impact of inflation is the net outcome of all of these gains and losses experienced by different groups of income recipients, by debtors and creditors, by workers and shareholders, by the owners of real and financial assets and by various other groups.

What is the significance of these redistributive effects? Does inflation rob the rich to pay the poor or does it rob the poor to pay the rich? Some economists believe that it can shift income and wealth about in either direction, depending on circumstances. They emphasize the unplanned and haphazard nature of the redistributive effects, which in so far as they have any systematic 'net' impact on the distribution of income and wealth are as likely as not to leave it less rather than more equitable. Baumol and Blinder exemplify this view: 'Why, then, is the redistribution caused by inflation so widely condemned? Because its victims are selected capriciously. Nobody legislates this redistribution. . . . The gainers do not earn their spoils, and the losers do not deserve their fate. . . . This is the fundamental indictment of inflation' (1988, p. 104). Other economists are of the opinion that inflation does have a predictable effect on the distribution of income and wealth, tending to rob the rich to pay the poor. Fender, for example, concludes that there is 'evidence . . . that the upper income groups are particularly badly hit by inflation' (1990, p. 75). Members of right-wing political parties tend to be more concerned about inflation than members of left-wing parties (Mueller, 1989, pp. 286–91), perhaps because they own more financial assets whose real value is threatened by inflation (Minford and Peel, 1981).

It is clear that there are two main questions to be resolved. The first is simply: What *are* the redistributive effects of inflation? The problem here is to identify and explain the various channels through which inflation shifts income and wealth from one social group to another. The second question is: Do these effects have a recognizable overall impact on the distribution of income and wealth and, if so, what are its direction and magnitude? In other words, does inflation tend to reduce or to increase inequalities in the distribution of income and wealth and, if so, to what degree? These are the main issues in the contemporary debate among economists about the redistributive effects of inflation.

The interpretation of the inflationary process as incomplete voluntary indexation (see Chapter 3) provides a perspective from which to evaluate the standard arguments for believing that inflation redistributes income and wealth. Among the many ways in which income and wealth are redistributed during inflation are those that affect individuals and groups in the private sector as they receive and spend their incomes. For example, it would be unlikely that all households experienced the same rate of price inflation, and even if they did wages would almost certainly rise more quickly for some households than for others. The next step is to analyse the redistribution during inflation of wealth, the stock of assets owned by a household, as distinct from income, the flow per period of time of money or benefits in kind received by it. It is generally argued for example that inflation benefits debtors at the expense of creditors. The final stage is to introduce the biggest debtor of all – the government. Unanticipated inflation distorts the redistributive impact of taxation and public expenditure in several ways, for example by reducing the real burden of public sector borrowing.

10.2　THE REDISTRIBUTION OF INCOME DURING INFLATION

Inflation redistributes current incomes within the private sector in three ways, because (i) the prices of various goods and services rise at different rates; (ii) average incomes and the general level of prices rise at different rates; and (iii) the wages earned in various occupations, and the incomes received in other ways, rise at different rates.

The main problem in evaluating the real world significance of these effects is to disentangle the impact of inflation from that of the real market forces of supply and demand. For these forces influence the extent to which a particular social group can reverse the redistributive effect of a price or wage rise which benefited another social group. Even in a world of zero inflation, where as many prices were rising as falling so that the average level of prices was stable, *relative* prices would be continually varying to register constantly changing relative scarcities, constantly changing conditions of supply and demand. Some of the income redistribution that occurs during inflation is the by-product of properly functioning markets rather than a distortion of market outcomes caused by inflation (see Chapter 3).

(i) Prices Rise at Different Rates

Some households enjoy a favourable redistribution of income during inflation simply because the prices of the goods and services they buy rise more slowly than those of the goods and services other households buy. Real income decreases if either money income falls while prices are unchanged or prices rise while money income remains constant. Suppose that prices are rising but money incomes are static. If household A buys goods that are rising in price at an average rate of 10 per cent and household B buys goods that are rising in price at an average rate of 20 per cent, A's real income is falling at only half the rate of B's. So A ends up better off in real terms, as if during a period of stable prices A's money income had increased at twice the rate of B's. The fact that not all prices rise at the same rate is enough to redistribute real income among households. The next question is whether this effect is of any significance in the real world. Does the variance of individual price rises around the RPI or CPI average redistribute income between identifiable groups of households? If so, what is the size of the redistributive effects?

For the UK a piece of research by Fry and Pashardes (1985) suggests that there is an inflation bias of significant magnitude against low-income households and against large families. In order to test the hypothesis that households face different inflation rates because they purchase different baskets of goods, Fry and Pashardes look for correlations between actual disaggregated price indices and household characteristics such as expenditure level, family size, occupational category and unemployment. The disaggregated price indices show that during the period 1974–81 the lowest price rises were for items such as consumer durables which were bought mainly by higher-income households while the prices of fuels (except gas), which account for a bigger proportion of spending by low-income households, rose by 50–100 per cent faster than average. It is therefore clear that 'the major factor governing differences in the effects of inflation between households is their expenditure level, with price indices falling substantially as expenditure rises' (Fry and Pashardes, 1985, p. 25). The next most important factor was family composition, large families facing higher inflation rates. Occupational category and unemployment made little difference to the actual inflation rates experienced by households.

Moderate inflation appears to be a robber baron, taking from poor households by high price rises on fuel to give to rich households through low price rises for consumer durables. The scale of these effects, with the cost of living for low-income households rising approximately 5 per cent more than the RPI during the period 1974–81, implied 'continual erosion of the living standards of those least able to afford it' (ibid., p. 28). Here then, it might be inferred, is an egalitarian argument for eliminating inflation. Yet it is clear that the real culprit was not inflation, the sustained rise in the general level of prices, but the increase in the relative price of goods on which a typical low-income household spends a larger than average share of its budget. If the rise in fuel prices had not spread throughout the economy in increases in other prices and in incomes, the relative price change and its regressive redistributive impact would have been greater. Inflation in the mid-1970s worked as a kind of *ad hoc* method of indexing prices in general (and hence incomes, one person's price being another person's income) against the sharp rise in the price of a good of fundamental importance to most economic agents. So inflation, far from being the source of unfair redistributive effects, can on occasions be a mechanism for mitigating the redistributive impact of a change in relative prices caused by a disturbance in the conditions of supply and demand.

(ii) Wages and Prices Rise at Different Rates

Why do people worry about inflation? Perhaps the commonest cause of anxiety is reported by Brown (1985):

> There is probably a great deal in John Fleming's observation that people whose pay is revised annually are aware of the achieved revision only on one day in the year, and of the gradual decline of the purchasing power of their receipts throughout the other 364. (p. 336)

This commonsense insight underlies the wage lag hypothesis, according to which money wage increases tend to occur some time after price rises. Consequently, inflation is widely perceived as a threat to living standards. The wage lag hypothesis also implies that inflation increases the share of profits in national income to the detriment of the share accruing to wages.

This hypothesis raises two questions. Is there any reason in economic theory to believe that wage rises will consistently lag price rises during inflation? If so, does the hypothesis survive contact with the empirical evidence? Labour market imperfections such as annual wage settlements provide grounds for predicting that there will typically be a lag before workers secure higher wages to compensate them for higher prices. There is, however, an equally plausible story suggesting that in some circumstances price rises will tend to lag wage rises. It is helpful to recall the distinction between demand pull and cost push theories of inflation (Chapter 3). Wage lag is to be expected only under demand pull inflation. The initial effect of excess aggregate demand is to drive prices up, increasing profit margins and the cost of living before wages respond. So demand pull inflation tends to raise the share of profits in national income at the expense of wages. On the other hand, cost push inflation can be set in motion by wage rises, in which case profit margins shrink and the share of wages in national income increases before prices are raised. So economic theory is far from unequivocally endorsing the wage lag hypothesis.

Perhaps the empirical evidence can resolve the issue: Do wages in fact lag prices? An unanswerable question, unfortunately. The methodological problem is clearly stated by Kessel and Alchian (1960), who assert that for 'any time series of real wages, there exists a fantastically difficult problem of imputing changes in the level of real wages to one or the other of two classes of variables, i.e., real or monetary forces' (pp. 43–4). The problem is how to discover whether changes in real wage levels reflect (a) real economic forces, changes in such things as the supplies of labour and capital, the quality of the labour force, the pattern of final demand for goods and services (and hence the pattern of the derived demands for labour of different kinds); or (b) monetary forces such as lags in the inflationary process. It is obviously a case of looking for the closest correlation, but another problem immediately arises. The choice of when to begin and when to end the time series is arbitrary yet it can make all the difference to the result of the statistical test:

> By one selection of beginning and terminal points for an inflation it can be shown real wages fell; by another selection it can be shown that real wages rose. The fall in real wages reported by these observers is a product of the arbitrary way the time period during which inflation occurred was defined. (Kessel and Alchian, 1960, p. 64)

So the wage lag hypothesis has not really been empirically tested and a theoretical argument can be made against the inevitability of wage lag during inflation.

A final indirect test of the wage lag hypothesis is to examine trends in the shares of wages and profits in national income. The hypothesis implies that, other things being equal, the share of profits in national income increases during episodes of inflation. This is evidently not true of recent UK inflation (Table 10.1), high inflation in 1974–75 and 1980 being accompanied by low profit shares. But this is not enough decisively to reject the wage lag hypothesis, because other things were not equal. Perhaps the influence of inflation was overridden by the effects on profit shares of the recessions which coincided with high inflation in 1974–75 and 1980–81. Certainly profits tend to fall during a recession as output drops more than employment, bringing productivity down and hence increasing costs per unit of output (Black, 1985, pp. 79–81). There is another interpretation of events which is not rejected by the data. Brown conjectures that if 'wages . . . take the lead in inflation . . . it is to be expected that profit margins . . . will be at any rate temporarily reduced' (1985, p. 339). Wage push measured in terms of the increase in wages and salaries per unit of output was at its highest in 1974–75 and in 1980 (Table 10.1).

Table 10.1   Profits, wages, inflation and growth: UK 1973–83

	Gross profits/ GDP %	GDP deflator %	GDP growth %	Increase in wages and salaries/ unit of output %
1973	12.3	7.1	8.1	6.4
1974	8.9	14.8	−0.8	21.8
1975	7.9	27.2	−0.6	30.4
1976	8.4	14.9	3.9	9.9
1977	12.4	13.9	1.1	6.7
1978	13.0	11.1	3.0	11.4
1979	12.7	14.5	1.9	14.2
1980	11.9	19.8	−1.8	20.9
1981	11.7	11.7	−0.9	8.6
1982	12.9	7.2	1.4	4.1
1983	14.6	5.3	3.4	3.8

Source: Black (1985), Tables 8.2 and 20.2.

(iii) Wages Rise at Different Rates

As well as experiencing the 364-day decline in the purchasing power of their annually adjusted money wages, any group of workers in this position will also see other groups securing wage rises throughout those 364 days, some of them no doubt higher than they can hope for themselves. It is bad enough to face rising prices; to witness others winning the higher money wages to match adds insult to injury. In a world where money wages catch up with prices at different rates, inflation hits some people's standard of living harder than others and hence redistributes real income. For some economists this is the most serious adverse effect of inflation:

> This, I believe, is the true reason why inflation is damaging. It is most apparent in the deterioration of industrial relations; but it is not confined to that field – it extends much more widely. It extends, very importantly, to many kinds of public arrangements – pensions and social benefits on the one hand, taxes and fines on the other. In conditions of inflation these continually need re-fixing so that issues which had seemed closed have to be re-opened. All this is left out in the perfect flexprice model; but these are the ways in which inflation really hurts. (Hicks, 1974, p. 79)

So customary differentials between, for example, wages for skilled and unskilled jobs are disturbed by inflation, one group of workers gaining relative to the other. If labour markets were like daily auctions, wage rates would be fixed at the time of hiring each morning and could be quickly adjusted in the light of inflation. Any changes in differentials between the various occupations would reflect changing conditions of supply and demand and there would be no distortions caused by lags in inflation adjustment. In the labour markets of the real world, however, wage rates are not flexprices like auction prices but fixprices. Long-term contracts are commonplace and embody different adjustment mechanisms such as automatic indexation through a set formula or annual reviews with no guarantee of full indexation.

From the perspective of income redistribution the question is whether any regular pattern can be observed in wage differentials during periods of inflation and if so whether there is a theory capable of explaining the observed changes as the consequence of the inflation. There appears to be only one systematic pattern: inflation compresses differentials. According to evidence assembled by Mallier and Shafto, the twentieth century has witnessed a 'narrowing of occupational differentials' (1989, p. 239). Their explanation is that during a period of prolonged price inflation 'there has been considerable social and political pressure to raise the wages or maintain the real purchasing power of the "low paid" and restrain pay increases for the "well off" ' (ibid.). For example, Brown (1976) found that UK wage differentials compressed rapidly during the period of high inflation from 1972 to 1975. The redistributive significance of this movement in differentials is that the low-paid gain from inflation. However, the evidence does not establish that inflation *per se* is responsible for the narrowing of wage differentials.

The problem once again is that of isolating the effects of inflation from those of real economic forces and in this case from those of government policy. As Mallier and Shafto observe, a 'similar contraction in pay differentials has also taken place during periods of low unemployment' (1989, p. 239). This weakens the significance of the association between inflation and the compression of differentials because, in accordance with the basic Phillips relationship, inflation is frequently accompanied by low unemployment (see Figure 3.2). So it is impossible to say whether it is inflation or low unemployment which compresses differentials. True, wage differentials narrowed in the UK during the stagflationary 1970s when inflation was accompanied by *high* unemployment. However, the compression of differentials appears to have been the consequence of the prices and incomes policies which were in force at that time, so the redistribution of income towards the low-paid was the result of government policy rather than inflation.

To sum up, much of the unplanned and arbitrary income redistribution commonly ascribed to inflation is in fact the distributional side-effect of changes in relative prices or the conscious product of government policy. What is more, the inflationary process is itself an impromptu exercise in indexation by which the distributional impact of unanticipated relative price changes is moderated.

10.3 THE REDISTRIBUTION OF WEALTH DURING INFLATION

In reality households obviously do not spend all and only their current incomes on consumption; some spend more than their current income, some less. This permits the acquisition of real assets and the accumulation of financial assets – and liabilities. First, people might buy real assets – such as houses, works of art, classic cars, antiques and jewellery – for enjoyment of ownership over an extended period of time and perhaps with the object of selling later at a profit. Changes in the prices of these assets relative to the prices of goods and services in general will make their owners better or worse off in comparison with people who do not hold any wealth in this form. Second, some households might choose to save some of their income to accumulate a stock of financial assets such as cash, bank and building society deposits, equities and government bonds. In this way they become creditors, lending their savings via financial intermediaries to other households, and firms, who wish to spend some of their expected future income now by borrowing, thereby becoming debtors.

Real Assets

Real assets such as works of art, antiques, and sometimes even houses, which are in limited supply tend to rise in price more rapidly than most goods and services. Owners will find that the real value of their wealth has actually increased during inflation; if they were to sell their assets they could buy more with the proceeds than they could have done before the inflation. But is this necessarily the effect of the inflationary process?

The appreciation of a real asset during a period of inflation is the consequence of inflation only if it was inflation that caused the increase in demand which in turn caused the price rise in real terms. A painting by a struggling unknown artist bought for £50, or the equivalent of a pair of trainers, might have appreciated ten inflationary years later to £1 million, or the equivalent of a mansion in the country. But this is not entirely the effect of inflation; it is at least in part a straightforward example of supply and demand. The picture increased in *relative* value because of the growing fame of the artist. For the relative price rise to be the effect of inflation the relevant increase in demand must itself be caused by inflation. In other words the asset must be an 'inflation hedge', something bought with the specific aim of owning something that will outstrip the average inflation rate. Ordinary speculative buying is not enough; that makes sense under stable prices or even deflation if the nominal price of the asset is expected to remain unchanged while other prices are falling. For real asset appreciation to be the effect of inflation, the first move in the causal sequence which ends in rising relative prices of real assets must be fear of inflation. The importance of such 'inflation hedging' in the determination of real asset prices is not known. However, it is clear that the attractiveness of real assets as inflation hedges is undermined to the extent that financial assets, the only alternative store of wealth, are inflation proofed.

Of course the price of a real asset can go down as well as up. For example the fall in the price of commercial land was one cause of the decline in the wealth of the richest segments of society in the early 1970s (Table 10.2).

Table 10.2   Distribution of wealth: UK 1971–76

	1971	1976
Percentage of wealth owned by:		
Most wealthy 1% of population	21	14
Most wealthy 5% of population	37	27
Most wealthy 10% of population	49	37
Most wealthy 25% of population	72	61
Most wealthy 50% of population	89	85

Note: Ownership of marketable wealth plus occupational and state pension rights.

Source: CSO, *Economic Trends*, 1985.

Financial Assets

At the other extreme from the rational investor in inflation hedges is the person whose wealth is held in the form of cash. The £1 000 that Mr Miser keeps in a shoebox on top of the wardrobe will not buy in December the goods he could have purchased with it at the start of the year. Mr Miser's neighbour Mr Loser adopts a more sophisticated but far from foolproof approach to storing wealth, lending Mrs Winner £100 for one year at an interest rate of 10 per cent. Unfortunately for him prices rise by 20 per cent during that year, which means that Mr Loser has effectively *given* Mrs Winner £10. Mrs Winner paid a total price, including the cost of credit, of

£110 for goods which, had she saved up for them, would have cost £120 at the end of the year. Unanticipated inflation redistributes wealth from creditors to debtors because the rate of interest is negative, that is, lower than the rate of inflation.

Consequently, far from worrying about inflation, some people welcome it. Someone who takes out a long-term loan such as a mortgage finds that a period of price and wage inflation soon reduces the real burden of the debt. For example, price levels tripled in the US between 1966 and 1986, so someone who took out a mortgage of $6 000 in 1966 would have found the debt had fallen to $2 000 in real terms 20 years later. In this case inflation redistributes wealth from people who save by holding financial assets such as deposits with savings and loan institutions (thrifts) or building societies in favour of people who borrow those deposits in the form of mortgages, especially when the properties bought on those mortgages rise in price relative to other goods and services over the long term.

How important is this redistributive effect likely to be? For the UK, Foster (1976) estimated that between 1961 and 1974 £3 billion was redistributed from building society depositors to mortgage holders. This calculation compares actual interest rates, which were sometimes negative, with the hypothetical situation in which the inflation that occurred between 1961 and 1974 was fully anticipated in a real interest rate of 2 per cent, that is a nominal rate which was always 2 per cent higher than the inflation rate. The effect on the distribution of wealth was almost certainly regressive because the building society depositors (the creditors) were likely to be older and less affluent than the mortgage holders (the debtors). However, there are grounds for questioning the significance of this result.

Some economists claim that inflation causes a decline in the wealth of the most affluent sections of society (see Higham and Tomlinson, 1982, p. 8). And there is no doubt that the share of the UK's wealth owned by those groups declined sharply during the inflationary years of 1971–76 (Table 10.2). It appears that the redistributive effect observed by Foster (1976) has been over-ridden. Many households are both debtors and creditors and on balance it is the most wealthy ones which are net creditors with most to lose from inflation. It is obviously not unusual for a household to have both a mortgage and a building society deposit.

During its life cycle a household may move from net debtor status on taking out a mortgage to being a net creditor once this has been repaid. In any case other financial assets such as government securities and stocks and shares account for a larger share of wealth and are owned predominantly by the most affluent households. Accordingly the main redistributive effect of the unanticipated inflation of the early 1970s in the UK was a *progressive* redistribution of wealth. The fall in the value of financial assets was probably the most important effect of inflation on wealth in the early 1970s and explains much of the reduction in inequality that occurred during those years (Table 10.2). So inflation *did* have a systematic effect on the distribution of UK wealth in the early 1970s.

The question is: Why did the owners of financial assets not protect them against inflation? Why did they not succeed in reversing the redistributive effect of the original non-inflationary price rise at least to the extent achieved by other earners of income and holders of wealth? The answer appears to be that the inflation of the early 1970s was unanticipated, initiated as it was by 'the first oil price *shock*'. The degree to which inflation surprised owners of financial assets is indicated by the fact that for most of the 1970s real interest rates were negative (Table 10.3). In the 1980s, however, real interest rates were positive by an amount considerably in excess of the 2 per cent assumed by Foster (1976) to be the historical norm (Table 10.3). The owners of financial assets have slowly joined in the successive rounds of 'inflationary' price and wage increases that sought to reverse as far as possible the redistributive impact of the first 'non-inflationary' price rise. It is therefore unlikely that the effects of inflation on the distribution of financial assets are of permanent importance. Over time the losses suffered under unanticipated inflation can be recouped during the years when the general level of prices rises more slowly.

The redistribution of wealth within the private sector that occurs under inflation does not appear to be of both substantial magnitude and lasting duration. But what of the government?

10.4   THE GOVERNMENT

One of the principal aims of government activity is to redistribute

Table 10.3   Real interest rates: UK 1971–89

Year	Bank rate/RPI %
1971	−3.4
1972	−0.6
1973	−0.7
1974	−4.6
1975	−13.7
1976	−5.0
1977	−7.8
1978	0.7
1979	0.6
1980	−2.0
1981	0.1
1982	5.9
1983	5.4
1984	4.5
1985	5.9
1986	7.6
1987	5.3
1988	6.1
1989	5.0

Source: Wall (1990), Table 10.2, p. 26.

the incomes generated by market transactions in a progressive direction, that is to make the distribution of income more equal. This objective is pursued in three ways: (i) through a progressive tax system which captures a greater proportion of high incomes; (ii) by paying cash benefits to the old, the unemployed and others; and (iii) by providing benefits in kind such as education and health care free at the point of consumption.

The standard view of the impact of inflation on these activities is that the government, as the largest debtor in the economy, is the greatest winner from unanticipated inflation. Thomas, for example, concludes that in the UK 'the personal sector has consistently lost out to the government' (1986, p. 29). The empirical evidence certainly seems to support this verdict (Table 10.4). Similarly, Dornbusch and Fischer argue that in the US 'an inflation rate of 5 percent in 1985 would have resulted in a transfer of $75 billion from the household sector to the government' (1987, p. 565). A little logical analysis reveals these claims to be meaningless.

Table 10.4   *The effect of inflation on nominal asset holdings: UK 1974–82*

Sector	1974	1976	1978	1980	1982
Personal	−10.7	−9.3	−7.0	−13.6	−7.6
Company	3.0	1.5	0.9	0.8	1.0
Public	9.3	7.5	6.7	13.1	7.3

Source: Bank of England (1984).

There is nothing wrong with the standard explanation of the mechanism which transfers real resources from the personal or household sector to 'the government', a device which is known as the inflation tax. The ultimate effect is as if the government had increased the rate of a conventional tax such as income tax or an expenditure tax. Suppose that the government increases the money supply in order to raise public expenditure on schools or hospitals. The central bank issues the new money and the government uses it to employ more teachers or doctors and nurses, to build more schools or hospitals, to buy more textbooks or stethoscopes. So stage one of the mechanism is that the government has increased its command over real resources. The increase in aggregate monetary demand causes an acceleration in the rate of inflation which, to the extent that it is not anticipated, reduces the real value or purchasing power of nominal assets such as cash and bank deposits held by the personal sector. So stage two of the mechanism is that the personal sector has lost some of its command over real resources. The conclusion is evidently that inflation has transferred purchasing power or command over real resources from the personal sector to the government.

But what does it mean to say that the government has increased its command over real resources? All that it means is that the government has removed purchasing power from the personal sector through the inflation tax and given it back to the personal sector in the form of higher public expenditure. Households sacrificed the consumer goods and home improvements and holidays they could have bought had their original purchasing power remained intact for the schools or hospitals that could not have been built without the revenue from the inflation tax. The point is that what a particular household paid in inflation tax is not necessarily the same as what it gained from using the new schools or hospitals. The inflation tax effected a redistribution of real resources that might not have been possible if only the more visible form of conventional taxation had been available.

The claim that the government is the principal beneficiary of the redistribution of real resources by inflation would make sense only if it were a final consumer of goods and services, as are households and firms. But it obviously is not. The government is simply a channel for the transfer of resources from one part of society to another. It does not buy the services of teachers or doctors and nurses for its own benefit, because it is not the sort of thing that could benefit from such services. The government buys those services only to provide them free at the point of consumption to households. The question is: Who are the ultimate beneficiaries and whose sacrifice of real resources paid for these services?

The impact of inflation on the distribution of real resources cannot be estimated until the answers to two more technical questions are known. First: What is the effective incidence of the inflation tax and how does it compare with that of conventional taxes? Second: Which groups of households benefit most from public expenditure on benefits in kind and in cash? If these questions were to be answered it would be possible to compare the redistributive impact of the inflation tax with that of conventional taxes. All that can be guessed in the present state of knowledge is that inflation, in so far as it has an adverse effect on the real value of wealth held in nominal assets, may be more progressive in its redistributive impact than conventional taxes, certainly those on expenditure. It *is* known that cash benefits and to a lesser extent benefits in kind are progressive in their redistributive effects. It follows that a policy of reducing both inflation (that is, the inflation tax) and public expenditure on such benefits is likely to have a markedly regressive effect on the distribution of real resources.

10.5 CONCLUSION

The redistributive effects usually ascribed to inflation are more properly the consequence of market imperfections and changing conditions of supply and demand, which influence the extent to which different social groups can reverse the unfavourable redistributive impact of the price rise that initiates the inflationary process. The inflationary process is itself responsible for redistributive effects only when the lags in the sequence of adjustments are sufficiently long to be a more powerful factor in explaining distributional changes than the original price rise. The reduction in the real value of holdings of financial assets by the unanticipated inflation of the early 1970s appears to exemplify this genuinely inflationary redistributive effect. What little is known about the redistributive impact of the inflation tax suggests that moderate inflation with relatively buoyant public expenditure is significantly more progressive in its effect on the distribution of real resources than a policy of cutting both inflation and public spending.

11. The Output Costs of Moderate Inflation

11.1 THE GOAL OF PRICE STABILITY

Macroeconomic policy in the UK and US throughout the 1980s was based on the assumption that market economies cannot work efficiently without stable prices. Reagan and Thatcher put the elimination of inflation above all other macroeconomic goals, pursuing it even at the cost of falling output and rising unemployment. Price stability was supposed to transform and revitalize the economy, with benefits so great that almost any short-term sacrifice was worth making.

The aim of this chapter is to debunk this central objective of Conservative economics. It will be argued that the overriding importance of eliminating inflation is an arbitrary dogma with no basis in the facts. The benefits of price stability are the monetarists' holy grail, a vessel believed to be of miraculous power and sought with fanatical disregard for the consequences of the quest – but never found because it does not exist.

A number of arguments are advanced in support of the claim that moderate inflation incurs substantial output losses, revolving around the concepts of shoe leather costs, menu costs, international competitiveness and inflationary noise. These will be critically examined in turn, starting with shoe leather costs because this appears to have held the greatest appeal for mainstream economists for most of the postwar period.

11.2 THE MONETARY OR SHOE LEATHER COSTS OF INFLATION

For most of the postwar period economists' standard answer to the question 'What's wrong with inflation?' was 'Shoe leather and menu costs'. According to Bootle (1981), shoe leather costs were 'an aspect of inflation on which an enormous research effort has been lavished. In many studies, losses from this source constitute a large part of the total losses from inflation' (1981, pp. 38–9). Similarly, Smithin comments that for '25 years or so this was the standard theoretical case of the economists against inflation' (1990, p. 142). The so-called shoe leather costs are the obvious starting point for a critical survey of the output costs of moderate inflation. It will be argued that, despite their appeal to economists, these costs do not represent a serious loss to the economy from *moderate* inflation.

Three factors account for the appeal of shoe leather costs to economists. The first is that shoe leather costs are believed to arise even and indeed *only* if inflation is perfectly anticipated. This is what happens. People are accustomed to holding a certain quantity of real balances, which are simply cash and current account (or sight) deposits expressed in terms of their purchasing power, that is, adjusted for inflation. These balances must be presumed to yield utility, such as the convenience of having cash or cheques available for financing routine transactions. Otherwise no one would hold them, for doing so incurs an opportunity cost, namely the interest which could have been earned by transferring the money to a deposit account (or time) deposit. Since the nominal interest rate rises to compensate depositors for antici-pated inflation, people have an incentive to economize on real balances. For example, suppose that the nominal interest rate is 3 per cent when prices are stable and rises to 13 per cent when inflation is 10 per cent. Money placed on time deposit therefore grows in line with inflation, preserving its purchasing power, while a given sum of money in cash or a sight deposit will exchange for fewer and fewer goods as prices go on rising. So people will prefer to build up time deposits, keeping their holdings of cash and sight deposits to the minimum required to service their everyday transactions. The problem is that this involves sacrificing some of the utility they used to get from holding cash and sight deposits. It is this lost utility which constitutes the shoe leather costs of inflation.

This lost utility introduces the second reason for taking shoe leather costs seriously, which is that there appears to be a theoretical justification for them based upon the familiar concept of consumer surplus. Microeconomic analysis implies that in principle there must be a welfare loss from economizing on real balances. In Figure 11.1, the demand curve LL shows that the demand for real balances M^1 is high when the interest rate is low at r^1, interest on time deposits being the opportunity cost of holding real balances. The consumer surplus from holding M^1 real balances, shown by r^1LA, is the utility they yield in excess of their cost, that is, the interest forgone when the interest rate is r^1, shown by Or^1AM. If the interest rate rises during inflation to r^2, holdings of real balances fall to M^2 and consumer surplus equal to BAC is lost. It is that triangle which represents the shoe leather costs of inflation. What does this lost consumer surplus mean in terms of people's economic well-being?

This is where the third factor in the appeal of shoe leather costs comes in, because there is no doubt that in certain circumstances these costs are of the greatest possible significance. Under hyper-inflation the efforts of people to economize on real balances

Figure 11.1   The shoe leather costs of moderate inflation

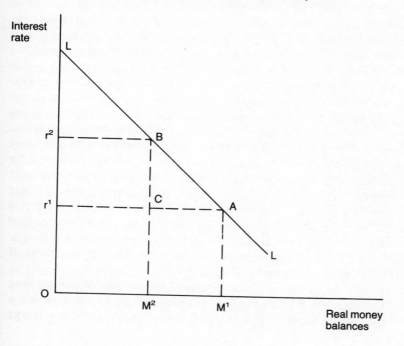

contribute to the collapse of the entire system of production and exchange. In the German hyperinflation of 1922–23, for example, holding cash even for half a day involved an intolerable loss of purchasing power, so shops closed in mid-morning as shopkeepers hurried to place the day's takings on deposit. The shoe leather used up in running to the bank several times a day stands for all the productive resources wasted in these sometimes frantic efforts to preserve the purchasing power of income. The wasted resources include not only the fuel and other costs of getting to the bank but also the labour unused and the capital equipment left idle while people who would otherwise be working stand in line to place their money on deposit. So it appears that there is empirical evidence to support a valid theoretical argument that even perfectly anticipated inflation incurs significant costs. But wait a minute. The empirical evidence applies to the limiting case of hyperinflation. How serious are the shoe leather costs of moderate inflation?

Disillusion with shoe leather costs sets in as soon as attempts are made to measure them under moderate inflation. For the US, Tobin (1972) reports an estimate that 'an extra percentage point of anticipated inflation embodied in nominal interest rates produces in principle a social cost of $\frac{2}{10}$ of 1 per cent of GNP per year' (1972, p. 15). To put this in perspective, an inflation rate of 40 per cent would be needed to cause an output loss of 8 per cent of GNP, which was estimated to be the output cost of US unemployment in 1982. For the UK, Minford and Hilliard (1978) produced results which suggest that the shoe leather costs of inflation at the rates actually experienced in the 1970s might not be negligible (Table 11.1). Even so, it would need an unemployment rate of only 5 per cent (or about half the rate experienced from 1983 to 1987) to cause output loss on the same scale as 30 per cent inflation. Moreover, these results appear to be a serious overestimate of the shoe leather costs of moderate inflation under contemporary financial institutions.

This claim rests on a theoretical assumption about the marginal cost of creating new bank deposits and on an understanding of the effects of financial deregulation in the 1980s. Minford and Hilliard (1978) made the standard assumption that the marginal cost of creating a new sight deposit is zero, or close enough to zero not to matter. All it takes is a few moments of computer time to set up a new account on the files. In effect, the production of sight

Table 11.1   *The monetary costs of inflation in the UK*

Expected inflation rate (%)	Welfare loss as percentage of GDP		
	$r^0 = 1\%$	$r^0 = 3\%$	$r^0 = 5\%$
2	0.04	0.08	0.12
4	0.12	0.20	0.27
6	0.23	0.35	0.47
8	0.39	0.55	0.70
10	0.59	0.78	0.98
15	1.24	1.54	1.83
20	2.15	2.54	2.93
25	3.30	3.79	4.28
30	4.69	5.28	5.87

Note: r^0 = the real rate of interest.

Source: Minford and Hilliard (1978).

deposits or current accounts is costless. The consequence is that the area Or^1AM in Figure 11.1 does not stand for the resources devoted to their production. Instead, the whole of the area under the demand curve LL represents consumer surplus. It follows that when inflation drives up the interest rate to r^2 the loss of consumer surplus is shown not by the triangle BAC but by the much larger area M^2BAM^1. It is this area which Minford and Hilliard (1978) attempted to measure.

In doing so, they overestimated the shoe leather costs of moderate inflation. The first point is that the standard assumption about the marginal cost of creating a sight deposit applies equally to time deposits. These are also effectively costless to produce. The second point is that financial deregulation has led to the introduction of deposits which combine facilities for cheques and immediate cash withdrawal with the earning of interest. So it is not always true that in economizing on cash and sight deposits people are losing the utility of cheques and immediate cash withdrawal. They may instead be switching to a new product which costs no more to produce yet allows instant access to funds while protecting their purchasing power against inflation. The nature of real balances has changed to encompass deposits with advantages previously found only in time deposits.

There are two ways of thinking about the implications of financial innovation for shoe leather costs. One is to suppose that all 'time' or interest-bearing deposits are modified to allow cash to be withdrawn and cheques written without notice. If everyone then switched out of old-style real balances to these new deposits, they would hold M^1 new-style or inflation-protected real balances with no change in consumer surplus and hence no shoe leather costs. Another way of looking at it is to suppose that *all* 'sight' deposits or current accounts earned interest. People would hold an unchanged quantity of real balances during inflation, and shoe leather costs would again be zero. In reality, the only people who would lose consumer surplus during inflation would be those who failed to make use of the new financial products and continued to economize on non-interest-bearing sight deposits in order to switch to old-style time deposits. However, as Bootle remarks, 'we can be sure that if interest rates in the UK ever reached the level of 30 per cent mentioned by Minford and Hilliard, interest *would* be paid on current accounts' (1981, p. 41). Shoe leather costs are therefore unlikely to amount even to the relatively low levels suggested by Minford and Hilliard (1978).

11.3   THE NON-MONETARY OR MENU COSTS OF INFLATION

Menu costs have two things in common with shoe leather costs: they are incurred even if inflation is perfectly anticipated and they have an intuitive appeal based on the behaviour of economic agents under hyperinflation. Even if inflation is perfectly anticipated, it cannot leave *everything* as it is; by definition, nominal prices change. Or rather economic agents change nominal prices and in doing so they employ scarce resources in a way that does not appear to be productive. For example, under hyperinflation people eating out might pay for their dinner in advance because they expect the restaurateur to raise his/her prices during the course of their meal. No more meals are being produced but costs have risen because labour, ink and paper are used up in revising the menu. The same is true of catalogues, price tags, vending machines and so on. However, Smithin expresses what is probably a common initial reaction in commenting that 'it is hard to see how these costs could really be all that significant' (1990, p. 144).

Minford and Hilliard (1978) offer a reason for taking menu costs more seriously. There is one price, the price of labour, which is not so easily revised. Adjusting nominal wage rates is not like rewriting a menu; a potentially lengthy and acrimonious process of negotiation is involved. In attempting to measure the non-monetary or menu costs of moderate inflation, Minford and Hilliard calculated the number of days lost because of wage disputes as a proportion of total days worked in order to estimate the costs of wage negotiations. They analysed data from a representative manufacturing firm to work out the salary costs of those employees who were responsible for publishing price rises and the costs of printing new price lists. The costs of known inflation are the sum of the costs of adjusting wages and the costs of changing prices (Table 11.2). It is difficult to disagree with Bootle's verdict that 'these estimated losses, although not insignificant, are hardly substantial and . . . increase much less than proportionately with the level of inflation' (1981, p. 38).

Furthermore, as with shoe leather costs, there are reasons for believing that even this low estimate of menu costs exaggerates their importance. First, to the extent that inflation is anticipated

Table 11.2 The menu costs of moderate inflation: UK 1976

Annual inflation rate (%)	Costs of known inflation (% GDP)
2	0.06
4	0.065
6	0.07
8	0.075
10	0.08
15	0.09
20	0.1
25	0.11
30	0.115

Source: Minford and Hilliard (1978).

firms will choose the method of disseminating price information
that minimizes the costs of changing prices. In Israel, for example,
many supermarkets code goods so that a computer can provide
the latest prices at the checkout (Brown, 1984, pp. 124–5).
Second, the assumption made by Minford and Hilliard (1978) that
wage disputes are entirely concerned with adjusting nominal wage
rates for price inflation is unconvincing. A firm might see inflation
as an opportunity to cut real wages, while union leaders aim either
to resist this or to press for an increase in real wages. Wage
negotiations ostensibly concerned with adjusting nominal wage
rates for price inflation may provide an arena for a struggle over
the relative rewards of workers and shareholders which would still
have to be resolved if prices were stable. So there is no good
reason for using the *total* number of days lost in wage disputes as
a proportion of the total number of days worked in calculating the
menu costs of inflation.

It may reasonably be concluded that the menu costs of moderate
inflation are much too small to contribute significantly to justifying
the goal of price stability.

11.4   INTERNATIONAL COMPETITIVENESS

The argument that inflation threatens the international competitiveness of industry is a long-established part of the anti-inflation
case. The declining competitiveness of UK manufacturing industry
has frequently been blamed on relative inflation, that is, a
domestic inflation rate higher than those of other industrial
countries. The broad empirical facts are consistent with this
proposition. The UK share of world exports of manufactured
goods fell from 20 per cent in 1954 to 9 per cent 20 years later
(Artis, 1986) and the UK inflation rate during that period was
higher than those of its major industrial competitors (Brown,
1985). The competitiveness argument has recently been put
forward with renewed urgency by business leaders in the UK.

In the autumn of 1990 Professor Douglas McWilliams, chief
economic adviser to the Confederation of British Industry,
launched a national campaign for stable prices with the claim that
'unless we change our inflationary habits, UK wages will overtake
German wages by 1995, with disastrous consequences for the

ability of UK firms to compete in world markets' (*The Independent*, Wednesday, 5 September 1990). This statement can be challenged immediately on two grounds. First, since the problem is *relative* inflation not inflation as such, international competitiveness does not require stable prices unless these have already been established in the economies of the UK's trading rivals. Since zero inflation is nowhere to be found among the major industrial nations, international competitiveness is at most an argument for reducing the UK inflation rate to the average of the industrial world. Second, there is something odd about claiming that UK firms will be unable to compete against German firms once UK wages have overtaken German wages. The implication, of which Professor McWilliams is apparently unaware, is that German firms cannot now compete against UK firms because German wages are higher than UK wages. However, despite the fact that they pay lower wages, UK firms are *already* uncompetitive to the extent that the UK has a substantial trade deficit with Germany.

How can German firms hold on to their domestic markets and win export orders against UK firms when they pay higher wages, a position which, according to Professor McWilliams, should render them uncompetitive? The explanation is twofold: first, competitiveness depends in part on factors other than price, such as design, quality, reliability and after-sales service; and, second, price itself is influenced by factors other than wage rates, such as productivity and the exchange rate.

A price rise will almost always lead to lower sales but can increase revenue if the fall in sales is proportionately less than the rise in price; if, that is, the demand for the product is relatively price inelastic. It is clear that people are willing to pay a higher price for many manufactured goods if they are confident that they will thereby purchase a product of superior quality or design or one that will prove reliable in use and convenient to service and repair. These characteristics tend to reduce the price elasticity of demand for the good and there is also the phenomenon of price being perceived as an indicator of quality. Ironically, it is German, and also Japanese, firms which have been prominent in moving their products up-market in order to sustain a higher price and hence greater profits. In so far as many UK firms have been unable to pursue the same strategy, the problem may be the quality of their products rather than the prices they charge for them. Of course some goods appear to be bought and sold solely on the basis of price; one bag of copper sulphate is much the same as another, so competitiveness here surely means getting the goods to market as cheaply as possible. There is some truth in this point, but even buyers of homogeneous products in industrial markets do not ignore non-price factors such as promptness and reliability of delivery. It cannot be taken for granted that relative inflation in the UK and hence higher prices for UK goods automatically makes them uncompetitive.

It is not even true that relative inflation is the only factor affecting *price* competitiveness. First there is the question of productivity. Higher wages or earnings per head might be no more than the reward for higher output per head, that is, higher productivity. So price competitiveness will be unaffected by relative wage inflation provided that higher earnings and hence higher costs of production are matched by improved productivity. Until the middle 1980s the rate of productivity growth in the UK lagged behind that of the industrial world as a whole (Smith et al., 1982). In the early 1980s wages and salaries per unit of output were inversely related to output per person employed (Figure 11.2). In other words, productivity rather than straight wage increases accounted for much of the variation in the price of UK goods as they left the factories. It is therefore clear that, even if the UK's poor trade performance were to be blamed entirely on a lack of price competitiveness, the alleged price uncompetitiveness was not caused solely by relative inflation in the UK.

Explaining changes in the prices of goods leaving UK factories is not of course the whole story. The prices of such goods when they reach the shops and showrooms of the world will have been influenced by the sterling exchange rate. The sterling effective exchange rate measures the value of the pound sterling against a weighted average of the currencies of the UK's trading partners, the weight attached to each currency reflecting the extent of its use in transactions involving UK exports and imports. In the 1970s it fell from an average of 125 in 1972 (1975 = 100) to 81 by 1978, offsetting the effects of relative inflation and slow productivity growth. However, sterling's rapid appreciation to 105 in 1981, in combination with rising wage costs and poor productivity growth, reduced the price competitiveness of UK manufacturing industry

Figure 11.2 International competitiveness

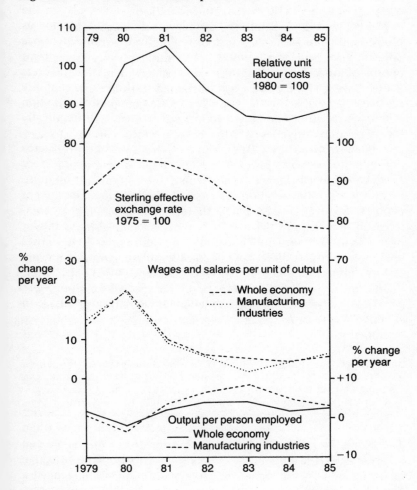

by approximately 50 per cent (Begg, Fischer and Dornbusch, 1991, Figure 29.5, p. 546). The most reliable index of international competitiveness is found by adjusting unit labour costs for exchange rate fluctuations to yield relative unit labour costs. The severe loss of competitiveness in the early 1980s is shown by the sharp rise in this index (Figure 11.2). Relative inflation does not appear to have exerted a dominant influence on the international competitiveness of UK manufacturing industry.

The entry of the UK into the exchange rate mechanism (ERM) of the European Monetary System nullifies one – but only one – objection to the international competitiveness argument. The option of offsetting a long-term upward trend in the prices of goods leaving UK factories by a sustained sterling depreciation is no longer available. In the context of ERM membership relative UK wage inflation and slow productivity growth *will* undermine the price competitiveness of UK goods in world markets. There is that much truth in the CBI's argument. But first, the problem is not inflation as such but *relative* UK wage inflation *plus* poor productivity performance, and second, the output and employment effects still depend on the price elasticity of demand for UK exports. So even in the ERM there is no direct link between inflation in itself and the loss of output and employment. Moreover, the deflationary policies needed to restore price competitiveness may involve a direct cost of considerable magnitude in terms of lost output and employment (see Chapters 14–16).

The limitations of the international competitiveness argument as a justification for seeking to eliminate inflation can best be summed up by considering a comment on a leading German car manufacturer:

> BMW's biggest long-term threat is its continuously rising costs. This is a particularly serious problem because BMW produces most of its cars in high labour cost countries such as Germany . . . and because export sales are increasingly affected by the strength of the German Mark against foreign currencies. (*CAR*, January 1991, p. 150)

There are two points of interest here. First, Germany's low inflation rate is legendary and yet labour costs in German manufacturing industry are higher than in most of its industrial competitors. For example, they are 75 per cent higher than in high inflation Spain (ibid.). Second, the strength of the Deutschmark is directly related to Germany's low inflation record, because a currency which is unlikely to lose value is obviously attractive to speculators. So the alleged benefits to competitiveness of low inflation are lost to some extent by a high exchange rate, while the penalties of high inflation can be offset by a low exchange rate.

Relative inflation can in certain circumstances make it harder for firms to compete in domestic and world markets but it is not the catastrophe the CBI appears to believe it to be.

11.5 PRICE SIGNALS AND INFLATIONARY NOISE

The last argument to be examined, the 'inflationary noise argument', holds a particular attraction for economists committed to the free market economy. It has been influential with Conservative politicians, and was cited as a major reason for defeating inflation by the Thatcher government in submissions to the House of Commons Treasury and Civil Service Select Committee (1980–81). None of the alleged costs of inflation so far considered is sufficiently serious to justify making price stability the dominant objective of macroeconomic policy. This means that the inflationary noise argument is the 'make or break' issue for those who believe in eliminating inflation whatever the consequences. It therefore merits lengthy examination.

The Alleged Effects of Inflationary Noise

The principal argument for price stability put forward by monetarist intellectuals like Tim Congdon (*The Independent*, 5 June 1989) is that without it the market economy cannot allocate resources efficiently. Markets coordinate the economic activities of individuals through the changing pattern of relative prices. Inflation introduces 'noise' into the economy, the upward movement of the general price level interfering with the transmission of information through changes in relative prices. Firms find it difficult to distinguish a genuine scarcity-signalling price rise from the persistent upward movement of prices in general, which is inflation. If, for example, a firm increases output in response to a merely inflationary price rise, the extra resources it uses will be misallocated. Moreover, Mr Congdon implies that even if the firm penetrates the 'noise' and realizes that relative prices have not changed, it will have used scarce resources such as skilled economists' labour in doing so.

It is worth examining more closely the ways in which changes in relative prices are supposed to influence production decisions. In the first place, producers respond to changes in the relative prices of the resources they use by switching to cheaper substitutes in pursuit of the least-cost combination of inputs. A major virtue of the market, according to Hayek (1945), is how little each buyer or seller needs to know in order for relative prices to disseminate information about relative scarcities. Suppose that tin becomes more difficult to obtain. No one needs to know *why*; all that is required is that consumers of tin know of the price rise. They can then economize on tin by using less or switching to a substitute whose price is unchanged. Second, producers respond to changes in the price of their product by revising decisions about how much of it to bring to market. A rise in the price of a particular good signals its scarcity relative to demand and in a properly functioning market economy prompts producers to increase its supply. In this way resources are channelled to the production of those goods consumers most want to buy. Finally, if the rise in the price of the good is sustained into the long term, it will attract new entrants into the industry, assuming there are no barriers to entry. Perhaps they know of unused resources which could be set to work producing the good, or they may be willing to invest in new productive capacity.

How is inflation thought to impair the efficiency of these ways of disseminating information about the relative scarcities of various goods and resources? According to Milton Friedman, as inflation rises, so does its volatility, with the result that 'an additional element' of uncertainty is, as it were, added to every market transaction' (1977, p. 466). Some prices rise more quickly than others, making for greater variability of relative prices. This might make it difficult to know whether to interpret a price rise as a scarcity signal or as part of the general upward trend of prices. For example, suppose that a firm buying tin is faced with a price rise by its usual supplier. Without further information, it risks wasting scarce tin (if the price rise was a scarcity signal) or needlessly economizing on tin (if the price rise was purely infla-tionary). A rational decision requires the expenditure of resources to discover the reason for the price rise, which is precisely the task that Hayek believes the market makes unnecessary. In principle, then, inflationary noise inhibits the clear reception of price signals. Moreover, there is some evidence to support the empirical foundation of the noise argument; the variability of relative prices does appear to increase as inflation accelerates (Fischer and Modigliani, 1986). Nevertheless, the noise argument is thoroughly unconvincing.

Empirical Evidence on the Inflationary Noise Argument

The main empirically testable proposition which the inflationary noise argument implies is not supported by the evidence. The prediction is that, in so far as firms are misled into switching resources away from profitable uses to produce goods for which there is no demand, inflation retards the rate of economic growth. Brown, however, concludes of inflation that even

> at very high rates, it has proved compatible with a remarkable growth performance in Brazil . . . and at rather more modest levels, still well above the world average over our period, it has gone with outstanding development in South Korea and impressive sustained performances in Spain, Portugal, Greece and Turkey. (1985, p. 363)

Similarly, a survey of 24 OECD economies found that high inflation countries performed just as well in terms of real GNP growth as low inflation countries (Table 11.3). There is therefore no empirical evidence for the claim that inflationary noise reduces the efficiency of the price mechanism and hence the rate of economic growth.

The Microeconomic Assumptions of the Inflationary Noise Argument

A close examination of the ways in which sellers actually make

Table 11.3   Inflation and growth in OECD economies 1960–73 to 1973–81

	Slowdown in GNP growth	
	Larger than median	Less than median
Rise in inflation		
Larger than median	5	7
Less than median	6	6

Source: Bruno and Sachs (1985).

pricing decisions reveals serious doubts about the microeconomic foundations of the inflationary noise argument. The way in which pricing decisions are made, and hence the way in which incorrect or 'noisy' price signals could come to be given, depends on the structure of the market. Two objections will be made to the noise argument, one applying to the theoretical world of perfect competition and the other to markets as they exist in the real world. It will be argued that under perfect competition prices are set in such a way that sellers could send out noisy signals; there is *that* much truth in the noise argument. However, the conditions of perfect competition itself prevent anyone from being fooled into mistaking the noisy signal for an indicator of greater scarcity. In the real world, markets are not perfectly competitive and prices are commonly set on a cost-plus basis. It will be argued that in these circumstances it is unlikely that sellers will send out noisy price signals.

The proponent of the noise argument tells the story of relative price variability like this. The price of tin goes up in May while the price of aluminium remains unchanged until September. The 'catching up' price rise then makes it clear that the relative scarcity of the two materials has not changed. In reality tin was not any harder to obtain than aluminium; the change in their relative prices just made it look that way. So buyers who switched to aluminium during the summer were using resources inefficiently, needlessly economizing on tin and wasting aluminium. However, the argument so far begs the question in assuming that there was no good reason for the different speed of adjustment in the tin and aluminium markets. In what circumstances could the rise in the price of tin relative to that of aluminium be inflationary noise rather than a scarcity signal? Political upheavals in tin-producing countries, mining disasters, technical difficulties or higher wage costs would push the supply curve upwards and to the left. All that seems to be left is a mistake by tin producers in formulating inflationary expectations.

It is easy to see how erroneous inflationary expectations could lead to a noisy price signal under perfect competition. Sellers are price-takers in that they can sell all that they can bring to market at the prevailing market price. How do they discover what the market price is? By trial and error. If for example the goods are not selling, the price is obviously above the market-clearing level.

Prices can be expected to be revised frequently in search of the latest equilibrium price set by the constantly changing conditions of demand and supply. Suppose now that a seller raises his/her prices on the assumption that consumers expect inflation of say 10 per cent whereas in fact other sellers and consumers expect inflation of only 5 per cent. A mistake about the future rate of inflation has led a seller in search of the market price to send an incorrect or 'noisy' price signal.

Yet this cannot lead to any misallocation of resources. Each firm in a perfectly competitive market is a price-taker, unable by its own actions (including its mistakes in attempting to anticipate inflation) to affect the market price of the good and hence the quantity of resources allocated to its production. By definition, consumers, having perfect knowledge of the market, will not be misled into believing the ill-advised seller's higher price to be a sign of greater scarcity. Knowing that goods of comparable quality are available elsewhere at a lower price, they will shun the overpriced goods and the consequent build-up of stocks will quickly provoke price cuts in search of the market-clearing price. So while there is a risk in the theoretical world of perfect competition that some price signals will be mere noise, empty of scarcity information, it is hard to see how they could have a significant effect on the allocation of resources.

The position is reversed in markets that exhibit some degree of monopoly power. In such markets unwarranted price changes *could* lead to a misallocation of resources but it is unlikely that price signals will be noisy. Firms are price-makers, able to sustain a price increase by reducing output. If tin producers raise their prices in May, consumers switch to aluminium even though tin is no less easily obtainable than it was before the price rise. However, the existence of monopoly power means that the noisy signal is not self-correcting, as it was under perfect competition. Instead of being guided towards the market-clearing price, tin producers restrict output to preserve the new price level. The demand for aluminium expands on the assumption that it is more easily obtainable than tin. For consumers, aluminium *is* more easily obtainable than tin – but only because tin producers are using their monopoly power to sustain a price rise initiated by mistaken inflationary expectations. In this way inflationary noise could create an artificial scarcity of some resources and an equally artificial demand for others.

There is good reason to believe, however, that in markets characterized by monopoly power there is little likelihood that pricing decisions will reflect incorrect inflationary expectations. The typical method of pricing in such markets is 'cost plus', where the price is set to cover costs of production and a profit mark-up is added. Three possible reasons for raising prices can be distinguished. First, a price rise to pass on a prior cost increase to the consumer is obviously a valid scarcity signal. Second, the firm raises its prices in anticipation of an increase in the cost of its resources which does not materialize. The price rise would still not be noisy if the firm was simply discounting the effects of an expected event, such as political upheaval, a war or a technical problem in supplier countries, which never actually happens. For the anticipatory price rise to be noisy it must be prompted by mistaken inflationary expectations.

So, third, the firm might raise its prices because it misinterprets inflationary noise in the economy as a whole as a signal of an increase in the demand for its own products. If the firm does no more than raise prices in line with general inflation, the relative price of its products remains unchanged. To give a misleading price signal to its customers, the firm must raise its prices by more than the current rate of inflation. This involves a contradiction. A firm would first have to observe, say, 5 per cent inflation and misinterpret this as a signal of greater demand for its products. It would then have to decide to raise prices by, say, 10 per cent. Why would it do that if it did not believe that 5 per cent was the *general* rate of inflation? The noise argument makes the self-contradictory assumption that the firm does and does not misinterpret the general rate of inflation. Moreover, it is unlikely that the firm would prefer to be guided by variations in the general level of prices rather than by its specialist knowledge of its own product markets. No rational firm is going to assume an increase in demand unless, for example, its stocks of finished products are being depleted unusually quickly.

Under perfect competition sellers might send noisy or inflation-distorted price signals but they would not thereby mislead consumers. In markets where some degree of monopoly power exists, consumers could in principle be misled by noisy price signals but sellers are unlikely to send any. The conclusion of this examination of the inflationary noise argument is that it lacks not only empirical evidence in its favour but also convincing theoretical assumptions about the way in which the price mechanism actually works.

11.6 CONCLUSION

Four reasons for believing that moderate inflation causes output loss have been critically examined and none has been found to establish that such output loss occurs on a substantial scale.

The shoe leather costs argument is the one that has had the strongest appeal for economists for most of the postwar period and at least has the merit of yielding an estimate of output loss that is not altogether insignificant. However, even assuming a real interest rate of 5 per cent, the estimated output loss associated with 10 per cent UK inflation is less than 1 per cent of GDP (see Table 11.1). For the US, the estimated output loss is 0.2 per cent of GNP per year for each 1 per cent of inflation.

The estimated output loss from menu costs is even smaller, at 0.08 per cent of GDP at 10 per cent inflation (see Table 11.2).

There is probably some degree of truth in the argument that, *ceteris paribus*, relative inflation threatens the international competitiveness of manufacturing industry. However, other things are never equal and relative inflation does not appear to be the principal factor in explaining trade performance. The most that this argument could establish is a case for reducing inflation in a high inflation country to the average rate of its industrial competitors, not a case for stable prices.

In recent years Conservative politicians and economists have increasingly relied upon the inflationary noise argument as the foundation for their goal of price stability. This argument lacks empirical evidence in its favour and appears to be based on insecure theoretical assumptions about the working of the price mechanism.

One final comment on the quest for price stability seems to be justified. Interviewed on British television after the change of Chancellor of the Exchequer occasioned by Mrs Thatcher's downfall, John Banham, Director-General of the CBI, said that 'the most important thing the new Chancellor can do for business is to squeeze inflation out of the economy once and for all' (*Business Daily*, Channel 4, 28 November 1990). This is a typical expression of a common assumption among businessmen and Conservative politicians, that once price stability is achieved it is bound to last for ever. However, what is thought of as something rock solid – price stability – is in reality the fortuitous and ephemeral outcome of a huge number of price changes. It is an essential requirement of the market economy that relative prices and hence nominal prices should continually change. An economy in which the inflation rate was zero because no nominal prices were ever changed would be a strange place, where year after year the same number of people satisfied the same number of wants from a constant supply of resources. Price stability, or zero inflation, actually comes about because price rises happen exactly to offset price falls. It is entirely mysterious why this accident of mathematics should be thought capable of transforming the economic fortunes of a nation.

PART III
The Relationship between Unemployment and Inflation

12. The Natural Rate of Unemployment

12.1 INFLATION AND UNEMPLOYMENT

Implicit in an investigation into the output costs of inflation is the idea that inflation causes unemployment. Obviously, if output is lower during inflation than it would have been under stable prices, jobs will be fewer. The previous chapter's critical examination of the putative output costs of inflation suggested, however, that the occurrence of such costs is uncertain and their magnitude negligible. But this is far from being the end of the claim that inflation causes unemployment, for there is another quite different line of thought that has led some economists to that conclusion.

This line of thought concerns the relationship between inflation and unemployment. The only account of this relationship so far considered is the Phillips curve, which represents the trade-off between inflation and unemployment that provided a framework for postwar demand management. Lower inflation could always be achieved but only at the cost of higher unemployment, and vice versa. The implication of this perspective on the relationship between inflation and unemployment is that, if the costs of each phenomenon are known, it is a simple matter to identify the optimal demand management policy. Does a one percentage point fall in the inflation rate 'save' more or less output than a one percentage point rise in the unemployment rate? And at what rate can lower inflation be traded off against higher unemployment – is it as simple as one-to-one or is a one percentage point rise in unemployment (inflation) enough to bring inflation (unemployment) down by several percentage points?

Here it seems is a framework waiting to organize the previous chapters' estimates of the costs of unemployment and inflation into policy advice. Suppose for example that moderate inflation does half as much damage as unemployment and there is a one-to-one trade-off between them. Then it is clear that people would be better off if the government were to reflate the economy to cut unemployment at the cost of a proportionate increase in inflation. The previous chapters have provided estimates of the costs of unemployment and inflation. Now all that is needed is to calculate the terms of the inflation–unemployment trade-off and a rational choice between reflation and deflation can be made. But it is not that simple.

The problem is that there are two other interpretations of the relationship between inflation and unemployment, according to which the trade-off is apparent only in the short run, roughly corresponding to a four-year electoral cycle. The central claim of the first of these theories, the natural rate of unemployment, is that over a longer period there is simply no trade-off at all between inflation and unemployment. At any stable rate of inflation, unemployment eventually returns to its natural rate. The second and distinctively Thatcherite view of inflation and unemployment is that in the long term the two phenomena can be seen to be *positively* associated, rising or falling together.

12.2   FRIEDMAN'S EXPOSITION OF THE NATURAL RATE OF UNEMPLOYMENT

The natural rate of unemployment was defined by Friedman as

the level that would be ground out by the Walrasian system of general equilibrium equations, provided that there is embedded in them the actual structural characteristics of the labour and commodity markets, including market imperfections, stochastic variability in demands and supplies, the cost of gathering information about job vacancies and labour-availabilities, the costs of mobility, and so on . . . (1968, p. 8)

Friedman used the concept of a natural rate of unemployment to support his argument that in the long run the Phillips curve is vertical, so there is no trade-off between inflation and unemployment. A moderate increase in inflation would, he thought, reduce unemployment in the following way: a monetary expansion increases the demand for goods and hence causes a general price rise; nominal wages respond more slowly and the consequent fall in real wages induces firms to move down their labour demand curves; unemployed people, anticipating stable prices, are willing to work at the unchanged level of nominal wages and so unemployment falls. This process depended on mistaken expectations about inflation. Once workers perceive the fall in real wages, they quit their jobs or negotiate for higher nominal wages. In either case unemployment returns to its original level while the new rate of inflation remains constant. The government, having sought to reduce unemployment at the cost of a moderate rate of inflation, is soon confronted by the original rate of unemployment in combination with the induced higher rate of inflation.

In the long run there is no trade-off between inflation and unemployment, and the rate of unemployment to which the economy tends to return whenever the rates of expected and actual inflation are equal is the natural rate of unemployment. In Friedman's analysis unemployment falls below the natural rate only if inflation is accelerating during each expansionary phase, so that expected inflation, which depends on past rates of inflation, is less than the actual rate. If the government reacts to this state of affairs by repeatedly expanding aggregate demand, inflation will accelerate while unemployment falls only temporarily. In this way repeated demand expansions in futile pursuit of an unemployment rate below the natural rate would induce higher and higher inflation rates with nothing to stop them culminating in hyper-inflation.

It is generally believed that the postwar Keynesian orthodoxy in demand management prevailed without encountering any real problems through the 1960s but was overturned by the stagflation of the 1970s, when the combination of accelerating inflation and rising unemployment provided empirical confirmation of Friedman's natural rate hypothesis. Against this consensus I will argue that the facts that are most convincingly explained by the expectations-augmented Phillips curve belong to the 1960s, and that it is of relatively little importance in understanding the 1970s.

12.3 THE POLITICAL BUSINESS CYCLE IN THE 1960s

There are two reasons for expecting Friedman's natural rate theory to throw some light on the 1960s. First, the behaviour patterns which Friedman ascribes to workers are plausible only on condition that the government is believed to be committed to full employment. Friedman's argument is that unemployment returns to its natural rate when workers voluntarily quit their jobs on realizing that their real wages are no higher than in the preceding period. It makes sense to assume that people voluntarily move in and out of employment in response to changing perceptions of real wages only if they can be confident of a continuing supply of vacancies. The UK unemployment rate was less than 4 per cent throughout the 1960s and governments were believed to be committed to full employment. In these circumstances people can reasonably be assumed to be likely to quit their jobs for repeated spells of frictional unemployment whenever they perceive their real wages to be no higher than in the previous period.

Second, the series of repeated reflations which Friedman postulates coincides with the political business cycle evident in that decade. Frey and Schneider (1978) tested the hypothesis that a rational vote-maximizing government will aim to expand the economy before an election, so that unemployment is falling but inflation rising, and deflate it after the election. An extra one percentage point on the unemployment rate was found to reduce the government's popularity by 6 per cent in the UK (1959–74), where monetary expansion preceded the elections of 1959, 1964 and 1970 (although not that of 1966) (Figure 12.1).

The natural rate hypothesis and the political business cycle

Figure 12.1   Money stock and elections: UK 1959–70

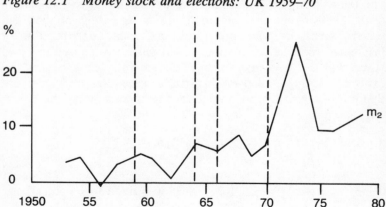

together imply that repeated monetary expansions to reduce unemployment before elections would in the long run induce higher inflation at the natural rate of unemployment. The empirical evidence fails to falsify this prediction. Since it is postulated that an unemployment rate regarded as electorally damaging prompted monetary expansion and any subsequent acceleration in the inflation rate, the unemployment rate for each year is plotted against the inflation rate for the following year. The Phillips curve plotted in this way by Brown (1985, pp. 226–8) can be divided into three short-run Phillips curves which shift upwards in time to the UK electoral cycle, and inflation and unemployment were both higher at the end of the 1960s than at the beginning (Figure 12.2).

The truth in Friedman's natural rate theory is that in certain circumstances demand management can be self-defeating. In the long run the Phillips curve will be vertical if, first, the government

Figure 12.2   Wage inflation, unemployment and elections: UK 1959–70

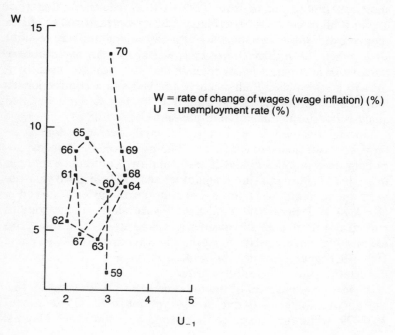

repeatedly reflates the economy to reduce unemployment before an election only to deflate it once the election is over and inflation is accelerating. Second, the expansionary phase of the political business cycle induces inflationary expectations in economic agents, which lead to voluntary job quits during the contractionary phase as unemployment returns to its natural rate at the new stable rate of inflation. The essential message of Friedman's natural rate hypothesis is simply that the perils of demand management are greatest when a government is close to its full employment target but wants to get even closer for political reasons. But a theory that warns against the temptations of success is not necessarily a reliable guide to misfortune.

12.4   THE STAGFLATIONARY 1970s

On the face of it, the empirical evidence offers some support to Friedman's expectations-augmented Phillips curve. Expansionary policies moved the large OECD economies north-west along a short-run Phillips curve from 1972 to 1973, causing a shift to a higher Phillips curve in 1974 (Figure 12.3). Contractionary policies then moved these economies south-east along this curve until 1978, when the process started all over again. An expansionary movement north-west between 1978 and 1979 was followed by a shift to a still higher Phillips curve in 1980 and a contractionary movement south-east along it until 1983. But a more detailed analysis overturns this initial impression.

Throughout the whole of the 1970s there were only four year-on-year movements that fitted a Phillips curve, the two expansionary ones in 1972–73 and 1978–79 and two contractionary ones in 1971–72 (of insignificant magnitude) and 1974–75. Two year-on-year movements were in a roughly north-easterly direction (1973–74 and 1979–80), implying outward shifts of the Phillips curve, and both were of considerable magnitude. Did those two expansionary movements along the Phillips curves of 1972–73 and 1978–79 trigger outward shifts of those curves? If so, was the expectations mechanism responsible?

A closer examination of the inflation of the 1970s suggests that the answer to the first question is yes for 1972–73 but no for 1978–79, while the answer to the second question is no. The first

Figure 12.3   *The Phillips curve in the large OECD economies:*
                1970–83

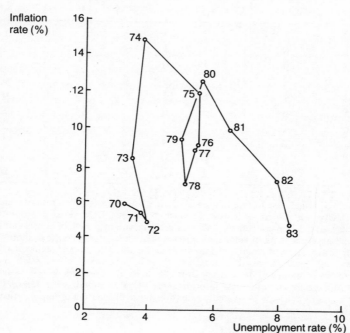

step is to isolate the demand pull and cost push components of inflation. Brown (1985, pp. 98–9) distinguishes four types of inflationary/disinflationary impulses: money injection, expenditure pull, wage push and import price cost push. The number of inflationary and disinflationary impulses of each type is recorded annually for eleven OECD economies. The results for the 1970s provide no support for the claim that rising inflation and unemployment were caused by repeated reflations. The monetary expansion in 1971–72, which foreshadowed the 1972–73 move north-west along the Phillips curve, is clearly indicated by 17 money injection impulses but after that *dis*inflationary monetary forces are dominant (Table 12.1). Moreover, there was no significant balance of inflationary over disinflationary expenditure pull impulses, except in 1976. The big outward shifts of the short-run Phillips curves coincided with 20 import price cost push impulses

Table 12.1   Inflationary and disinflationary impulses

Year	+M	+E	+W	+I	−M	−E	−W	−I
1970	2	1	3	3	5	3	0	1
1971	8	3	3	1	2	4	2	3
1972	9	3	1	0	0	1	2	2
1973	2	4	4	9	4	0	1	0
1974	1	3	6	11	6	5	0	0
1975	5	1	3	0	3	3	2	11
1976	1	6	1	4	4	2	7	2
1977	2	0	1	4	3	6	1	3
1978	4	1	0	0	5	1	4	8
1979	3	3	1	10	4	2	0	0

Note: +M = increase in rate of growth of broad money and fall in rate of increase of velocity; +E = increase in rate of growth of money GDP and rise in profit share of value added in manufacture; +W = increase in rate of growth of hourly earnings and fall in profit share of value added in manufacture; +I = increase of more than 1 per cent in rate of change of import price weighted by import share of GDP; −M = fall in rate of growth of money stock and rise in velocity; −E = fall in rate of growth of money GDP and fall in profit share of value added; −W = fall in rate of wage inflation and rise in profit share of value added; −I = fall of 1 per cent or more in a year in weighted rate of increase of inflation of import price (or similar rise in rate of decrease).

Source: Brown (1985), Table 4.2, p. 101.

in 1973–74 and ten in 1978–79. The greatest incidence of inflationary wage push impulses was also in 1973–74.

What seems to have happened is that expansionary monetary policies in the large OECD economies in 1971–72 increased the demand for and therefore the prices of primary products. The monetary expansion shifted the AD curves (see p. 19) of these economies outwards and to the right, implying higher inflation in association with higher output (and hence lower unemployment) and initiating north-westerly movements along their respective Phillips curves in 1972–73. The rise in primary product prices, especially oil, shifted their AS curves upwards and to the left, implying higher inflation associated with lower output (and hence higher unemployment) and shifting their Phillips curves outwards in 1973–74. There is no further cluster of money injection inflationary impulses after 1971–72 and in fact there were more disinflationary monetary impulses each year except 1975.

The only way in which these monetary injections could have initiated a cumulative inflationary process involves a more extensive role for expectations. When economic agents act on the basis of expectations they can in certain circumstances bring about the expected state of affairs. If consumers expect prices to rise, they will be willing to pay more for the same quantity of goods, shifting the demand curve upwards; if sellers believe that consumers expect price rises they will charge more for the same quantity of goods, shifting the supply curve upwards. Inflationary expectations are therefore sufficient in themselves to cause inflation. The question is whether they could have transformed the monetary expansion of 1971–72 into the sustained inflation that characterized the rest of the decade.

The belief that they could and indeed did is part of the second interpretation of the relationship between inflation and unemployment, according to which not only are they positively correlated, inflation actually causes unemployment. While this is *not* part of Friedman's natural rate theory, it is perhaps best understood as a distinctively Thatcherite development of it (Gowland, 1983).

12.5 DOES INFLATION CAUSE UNEMPLOYMENT?

Some people think we can choose between inflation and unemployment. Let inflation rise a bit they say to get unemployment down. But it doesn't work like that. The two go together. Higher inflation means higher unemployment. It's like an addictive drug, the more you need and the more damage it does to you. (Mr Geoffrey Howe, Chancellor of the Exchequer, Budget broadcast, 10 March 1981)

The sentence 'Higher inflation means higher unemployment' suggests that there is a causal relation rather than a mere statistical correlation here. Certainly, some Conservative politicians and monetarist economists see in this correlation the empirical confirmation of a theory that predicts that a rise in inflation *causes* a subsequent rise in unemployment. In fact the theory of the natural rate of unemployment does more than that, for it asserts that an initial rise in inflation will set off a cumulative inflationary process which, unless checked by government action, will culminate in hyperinflation. In the long run accelerating inflation will cause more and more unemployment until hyperinflation occurs and the economy collapses.

In the natural rate theory lie the foundations of the Conservative claim that the only valid goal of macroeconomic policy is the defeat of inflation. If it is true that inflation is the principal cause of unemployment, the battle against inflation is the decisive engagement in the campaign against unemployment. If inflation causes unemployment, the adverse effects or costs of unemployment *are* the indirect adverse effects or costs of inflation; if A causes B, and B causes C, C is simply the indirect or second-round effect of A. So the costs of inflation are necessarily at least as great as those of unemployment, since the former encompass the latter; it is not a question of which is the more serious problem, of whether the costs of inflation are greater or less than those of unemployment. And it is not a question of whether it is worth using a rise in inflation to reduce unemployment or cutting inflation at the cost of higher unemployment. There is no policy dilemma at all. Even if the ultimate objective of policy is to reduce unemployment, the essential first step is the elimination of inflation. If inflation causes unemployment, all roads converge on the route to stable prices. But does it?

12.6   INFLATION, UNEMPLOYMENT AND INFLATIONARY EXPECTATIONS

There is an argument derived from Friedman's analysis of the expectations-augmented Phillips curve which implies that in principle it could do so (Gowland, 1990, pp. 122–5). Inflation has two components: demand inflation caused by expansionary monetary policy, and expected inflation. The crucial parameter is the value of expected inflation. If expectations are based on past inflation, as Friedman assumed, there are three possibilities. First, the coefficient of expected inflation is greater than unity, that is, the expected inflation rate is higher than last year's actual inflation rate. In these circumstances monetary expansion causing demand inflation for a single year is enough to generate a cumulative inflationary process (Table 12.2a). This is the assumption about inflationary expectations that underlies the Thatcherite claim that inflation causes unemployment. Second, the coefficient of expected inflation is equal to unity, that is, expected inflation is the same as last year's actual inflation. Under these conditions a sustained monetary expansion year after year leading to a constant rate of demand inflation is necessary and sufficient to generate accelerating inflation (Table 12.2b). This is closest to Friedman's view of inflationary expectations and gives rise to the vertical long-run Phillips curve, which implies that there is no trade-off between inflation and unemployment. Third, the coefficient of expected inflation is less than unity, that is, expected inflation is less than last year's actual inflation. Increasingly large monetary expansions are now necessary to generate accelerating inflation (Table 12.2c).

Clearly, the isolated episode of monetary expansion in 1971–72

Table 12.2 *Demand inflation required to generate accelerating inflation under various coefficients of inflationary expectations*

(a) Coefficient of inflationary expectations = 2

Year	1	2	3	4	5
Demand inflation	2	0	0	0	0
Expected inflation	0	4	8	16	32
Actual inflation	2	4	8	16	32

(b) Coefficient of inflationary expectations = 1

Year	1	2	3	4	5
Demand inflation	2	2	2	2	2
Expected inflation	0	2	4	6	8
Actual inflation	2	4	6	8	10

(c) Coefficient of inflationary expectations = 0.5

Year	1	2	3	4	5
Demand inflation	2	4	8	16	32
Expected inflation	0	1	2.5	5.25	10.625
Actual inflation	2	5	10.5	21.25	42.625

Source: Developed from Gowland (1983), Appendix 4, pp. 114–16.

could have triggered the successive outward shifts of the Phillips curve later in the decade only if inflationary expectations had been based on past inflation with a coefficient of expected inflation greater than unity, that is if each year's expected inflation rate had been higher than the previous year's actual inflation rate. In these circumstances monetary expansion causing demand inflation for a single year would have been enough to generate successively higher rates of inflation at the natural rate of unemployment. The crucial question is whether the coefficient of inflationary expectations in the UK in the early 1970s was greater than unity.

Put like that, it is an unanswerable question. Measuring expectations is like measuring utility or any other state of mind such as boredom, toothache or happiness – impossible. Still, we *do* infer the strength of people's feelings from their outward behaviour, and econometricians have devised some ingenious ways of quantifying inflationary expectations, albeit indirectly. The consensus view appears to be that the coefficient of inflationary expectations in the UK in the early 1970s was less than unity, that is, that expected inflation was less than the previous year's actual inflation (Laidler and Parkin, 1975). The evidence fails to support either the Friedmanite 'no trade-off' thesis or the Thatcherite 'inflation causes unemployment' argument.

A more fundamental objection to the Friedmanite interpretation concerns the assumption that the coefficient of inflationary expectations is based entirely on past inflation. It is not necessary to endorse any formal version of rational expectations theory to find Friedman's model of expectations formation unconvincing, because it commits economic agents to making systematic forecasting errors. Since economic agents are by definition rational utility maximizers, expectations formation cannot be explained as a mechanistic process based on past inflation to the exclusion of other available information (Begg, 1982, pp. 22–6). So there is no reason to assume, as Friedman did, a constant coefficient of inflationary expectations and *a fortiori* no reason to believe that it is always greater than unity. That much seems to be clear.

As for the Thatcherite argument, it might be defended on the grounds that it is based on the assumption of rational expectations plus the empirical claim that throughout the 1970s it was rational to expect each year's inflation to be higher than last year's. However, it is clear that the government will not persevere with expansionary monetary policies after perceiving their inability to secure a permanent reduction in unemployment, and this change of policy will be incorporated into rational inflationary expectations. Inflation, being expected to fall, will do so. So the rational expectations assumption does not appear to offer a convincing defence of the 'inflation causes unemployment' argument.

Acknowledging the power of inflationary expectations, recognizing that 'expecting makes it so', is itself the quintessential Friedmanite insight.

12.7 CONCLUSION

Friedman was right about the importance of expectations in the cumulative inflationary process but wrong about the way in which such expectations are formed. The natural rate of unemployment and with it the expectations-augmented Phillips curve do not establish the claim that in the long run there is no trade-off between inflation and unemployment. Neither can they possibly provide a rational foundation for the Thatcherite fear of inflation as a cumulative process causing mass unemployment and culminating in hyperinflation. The stagflationary 1970s, far from confirming the natural rate hypothesis, terminated the brief period during which the outward shift of the short-run Phillips curve could plausibly be interpreted as the consequence of demand management policies on economies close to full employment. Unfortunately, policy makers did not act on the natural rate hypothesis until its reliability as a guide to policy had been destroyed by the first oil price shock.

13. Conviction and Consensus Approaches to Macroeconomic Policy Making

13.1 TWO INTERPRETATIONS OF THE NATURAL RATE OF UNEMPLOYMENT

The plan of this part of the book is to arrive at a reasoned conclusion about the relation between unemployment and inflation. It was argued in Chapter 12 that except in highly unusual circumstances inflation does not cause unemployment. But this leaves open the possibility that there is no trade-off between unemployment and inflation. If the Phillips curve is vertical in the long run, this might mean not that repeated reflations culminate in hyperinflation but that governments settle for the natural rate of unemployment out of fear of the inflationary consequences of trying to bring unemployment below it. But 'in the long run we are all dead'. Certainly, if the economy takes decades to reach equilibrium, the short run is all that policy makers ought to worry about. Is there a trade-off between unemployment and inflation over whatever period of time is deemed relevant for policy making and, if so, how much more unemployment must be tolerated to secure a given fall in inflation?

The aim of this chapter is to outline a theoretical framework for answering these questions. The idea of the natural rate of unemployment has been taken up, in one form or another, by most macroeconomists. Samuelson and Nordhaus, for example, conclude that the simple and stable Phillips curve has been replaced by the more subtle natural rate of unemployment theory (1985, p. 254). They believe that it is possible to ride the short-run Phillips curve, using a positive demand shock to drive unemployment temporarily below the natural rate at the cost of accelerating inflation, or a negative demand shock to reduce inflation at the cost of pushing unemployment above the natural rate. But in the long run there is no trade-off between inflation and unemployment. The expectations-augmented Phillips curve, and with it the natural rate of unemployment, appear to have become firmly established in mainstream macroeconomics. There are, however, two main interpretations of natural rate theory in current use which have radically different policy implications.

These two broad approaches to macroeconomic policy making are distinguished by their assumptions about the adjustments economic agents are likely to make in response to policy changes. Specifically, the question is whether agents respond to disinflationary policies by making price or quantity adjustments. New classical economists such as Matthews and Minford (1987) assume that markets clear; price changes without delay so that it is always at its equilibrium level and the quantity supplied can all be sold. In the extreme case disinflation can be achieved without any cost in terms of higher unemployment. Keynesians, in the broadest sense of those who see a role for demand expansion in reducing unemployment, believe that prices and wages are sticky and hence that quantities have to take the initial burden of adjustment to policy changes. So disinflation always involves a fall in output and a consequent increase in unemployment.

Suppose that the government implements a contractionary monetary policy aimed at reducing inflation. Economic agents respond either by cutting prices or reducing output and hence jobs, so that the aggregate outcome is a fall in inflation accompanied by an increase in unemployment. Clearly the terms of the inflation–unemployment trade-off, the amount of extra unemployment needed to secure the desired fall in inflation, depend upon the decisions of many individual economic agents. If most of them cut prices only slowly after promptly reducing output and shedding jobs, the unemployment cost of disinflating is high. If, on the other hand, most people cut prices at once, output and unemployment remain broadly stable and the disinflation is almost painless. What attitudes might policy makers adopt if experience shows that most people tend to adjust output and jobs first and ask questions about prices afterwards?

Two possible attitudes are conviction and consensus. Take two policy makers who share a commitment to price stability. So certain is Mrs Inflexible of the rightness of this goal that she is happy to pursue policies that inspire hostility and opposition, requiring a trial of strength or a test of nerve before people change their behaviour in ways that permit the policy to work. She therefore presses on with instant disinflation in the belief that the severe unemployment cost this time will produce a nation of price-cutters next time around. Mr Reasonable prefers to modify policy proposals so that they enjoy widespread support among the people whose interests are affected by them. Accordingly, he accepts the fact that people normally make quantity adjustments ahead of price changes and proceeds with caution, tightening monetary policy gradually so that people have time to cut prices and avert the worst of the unemployment consequences of disinflation. Corresponding to each of these attitudes, of conviction and consensus, is a distinctive understanding of the idea of the natural rate of unemployment and of the role of demand management.

13.2   EQUILIBRIUM UNEMPLOYMENT

The conviction interpretation is exemplified by Matthews and Minford (1987), whose concept of equilibrium unemployment, defined as unemployment which is not affected by demand shocks, is clearly descended from Friedman's natural rate of unemployment. What is new is their 'new classical' conviction that all unemployment is voluntary. New classical economists admit that in theory involuntary unemployment could occur in the short run. It would be caused by the existence of wage contracts negotiated by trade unions, which last long enough to prevent wage rates adjusting to clear the labour market. In other words, workers could not take a wage cut to save jobs even if they wanted to do so, because by the time their contracts were due for renegotiation their employers would already have made some people redundant. According to Minford (1985) however, there is a residual non-union labour market where wage rates are free to fall to eliminate excess supplies of labour, thereby clearing the labour market as a whole. Workers who lose their jobs in the unionized labour market can always take a drop in wages and find work in the non-union labour market. Consequently there is no involuntary unemployment, even in the short run.

The level of employment in the union sector E_u is measured from left to right (Figure 13.1). The union real wage rate W^u and

*Figure 13.1   Labour market clearing and equilibrium
                unemployment*

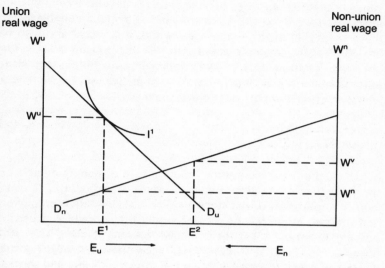

E_u = employment in union sector

E_n = employment in non-union sector

the level of union sector employment E^1 are determined by the
tangency of the union's indifference curve I^1 with the demand for
union labour curve D_u. According to Minford, the labour supply
curve intersects the demand for non-union labour curve D_n to give
a non-union real wage rate of W^n and a level of non-union sector
employment (E_n measured from right to left) of E^1, thus clearing
the labour market. A non-union wage rate of W^v would give non-
union employment of E^2 and hence voluntary equilibrium
unemployment of $E^1 - E^2$.

This is an economic theory of how the labour market works and
its proponents have what they see as good reasons for believing it
to be true. But it is a model that appeals to politicians whose
dominant attitude to people with different interests and beliefs is
one of confrontation based on complete conviction in the truth of
their own principles. If the labour market clears, all unemployment

even in the short run is voluntary. Unemployed people could have found work in the non-union sector of the labour market but opted instead for idleness supported by the efforts of others. The conviction politician seeks to change this behaviour by supply-side measures to reduce the value of unemployment benefits or to make them harder to obtain. Meanwhile, it is essential not to be misled by rising unemployment into relaxing policies designed to eliminate inflation. In this way equilibrium unemployment is the natural ally of a conviction policy objective of 'stable prices whatever the unemployment consequences'.

13.3   NAIRU

NAIRU, the non-accelerating inflation rate of unemployment, is the most firmly established interpretation of the natural rate. Its central implication is that since governments as well as employers and unions can affect the real economy they should proceed by building a consensus for their policies. Layard (1986) defines it in terms of the familiar Phillips relationship between inflation and unemployment. If unemployment is low, inflation will rise as employers pay more than the going rate in order to recruit workers, and unions feel able to push for higher wages. If unemployment is high, inflation will fall. Between these two cases, there is 'a critical level of unemployment at which inflation will be just stable – neither rising nor falling. We shall call this the NAIRU (the non-accelerating inflation rate of unemployment)' (Layard, p. 29).

NAIRU is determined in the labour market bargaining process. The feasible real wage depends on the living standard which the economy can provide. The pricing decisions of firms determine the real wage in the long run, because if unions press for real wages above the feasible level, firms will raise prices to offset increases in money wages granted in response to union pressure and so maintain real wages at their feasible level. NAIRU is the level of unemployment which is just sufficient to ensure that the target real wage aimed at by unions equals the feasible real wage. For example, if productivity growth fell the feasible real wage would also fall, causing NAIRU to rise, while if trade union power increased the target real wage would also increase and NAIRU would again be forced up.

The NAIRU method seems to have become established as the standard way of measuring the natural rate of unemployment. Layard and Nickell (1985) operate on the basis of changes between time periods, assuming that on average unemployment was at NAIRU during the first period 1955–66 and hence generating estimates for the remaining three periods, 1967–74, 1975–79 and 1980–83. The equation Layard and Nickell used in estimating NAIRU is derived from their unemployment equation, which, putting it as non-technically as possible, is of the form:

$$U = \sigma + K/L + Z + (P - P^e) + (W - W^e)$$

where σ represents deviations of aggregate demand (reflected in measures of fiscal stance and world trade) from its natural or full employment level, K/L is the ratio of capital to the labour force, Z is an index of wage pressure factors, P is the price level, P^e is the expected price level, W is labour costs and W^e is expected labour costs. Where do the values of these variables come from? What do they mean?

These variables can be estimated only indirectly and on the basis of questionable assumptions. The equation states that one of the determinants of unemployment is labour costs, specifically the difference between actual and expected labour costs, $W - W^e$. This embodies a model of wage determination according to which 'employers set employment (given the wage), and unions set the wage (given the demand curve for labour)' (Layard and Nickell, 1985, p. 68). Evidently Layard and Nickell need a theory of the firm from which to derive the demand curve for labour. So they 'suppose that the economy consists of a number (n) of identical imperfectly competitive firms' (ibid., p. 63) while admitting that 'in reality systematic changes in the degree of monopoly may have occurred' (ibid., p. 66). Production by imperfectly competitive firms depends upon the ratio of capital to labour, K/L in the equation, which raises further problems. Before 1958 the data on 'gross capital stock at 1975 replacement cost' was available only for 1948, 1951 and 1954, figures for the missing years being interpolated by calculations based on a different series, namely 'total gross domestic fixed capital formation'. Turning to the supply of labour, the value of the wage push variable, Z, will be higher if the unemployed are less willing to work, because this will reduce the supply of labour relative to demand and hence increase wages for a given level of unemployment. How hard the unemployed look for work presumably depends on the replacement ratio and also on such matters as 'reduced harassment at benefit offices, greater willingness to live off the state, reduced work ethic, and so on' (ibid., p. 69). Unfortunately, 'none of these factors can be directly measured' (ibid.). Enough. It is surely clear that measuring NAIRU is about as easy as drawing a black cat which, rumour has it, frequents a cellar at midnight, or more prosaically, that NAIRU is a 'prime example of a theoretical construct which . . . has no empirical counterpart' (Thirlwall, 1983, p. 179).

Considerable uncertainty surrounds the measurement and policy application of NAIRU. The unemployment equation implies that actual unemployment is influenced by demand factors and expectational errors about wage and price inflation as well as by the Z factors which determine NAIRU. The NAIRU equation is obtained by setting $P = P^e$ and $W = W^e$, so that neither prices nor wages are running ahead of expectations and demand is therefore at its natural level:

$$U^* = K/L + Z$$

Assuming that the capital stock has no long-run effect on unemployment, NAIRU depends upon the wage push factors Z, including the replacement ratio (the ratio of income when unemployed to income when in work), an index of trade union power, the ratio of import prices to domestic prices, and the mismatch between the skills of the unemployed and the requirements of job vacancies.

These wage push factors are influential in determining the target and feasible real wage rates. The natural rate of unemployment rises if an increase in trade union power raises the target real wage or if an increase in the replacement ratio reduces the feasible real wage. On the other hand, there is still room for an increase in demand deficiency unemployment caused by a fall in aggregate demand below its natural or full employment level. So governments ought to proceed cautiously, implementing only those contractionary policies for which a consensus exists if they wish to minimize the output and unemployment costs of disinflation.

This policy implication is reinforced by the long-run NAIRU incorporated in an imperfect competition model expounded by Davies (1985). Firms and workers alike face downward-sloping demand curves and therefore have to take account of quantities as well as prices. They would like to sell more at prevailing prices or wage rates but find that if they try to do so prices or wage rates will be forced down. In these circumstances changes in aggregate demand will affect output and employment as firms and workers make quantity adjustments, although eventually they will revise price and wage demands. The essential point in deriving NAIRU is that 'the mark-up charged by firms (P/W, where P is the average price level and W is the average wage level) is in fact the inverse of the real wage W/P demanded by workers' (Davies, 1985, p. 71). In the long run there is only one level of aggregate demand which can produce a mark-up P/W consistent with the real wage demands of workers W/P, and the long-run NAIRU is the rate of unemployment associated with that level of aggregate demand.

13.4 EQUILIBRIUM UNEMPLOYMENT VERSUS NAIRU

There are radical differences between these two interpretations of the concept of the natural rate of unemployment on matters of explanation and policy advice. Both interpretations share a negative understanding of the natural rate of unemployment as that part of total unemployment which cannot be eliminated by the expansion of aggregate demand. This reflects their common ancestry in Friedman's original concept of the natural rate of unemployment and the fact that that concept could almost be interpreted as another term for full employment. If the aggregate supply curve eventually becomes vertical, then it is obvious that the Phillips curve must also become vertical at the corresponding level of employment. Any residual unemployment would be frictional and voluntary. No matter how much aggregate demand was expanded and inflation increased, unemployment would not fall any further. But the point is that full employment is a desirable state, and hence an objective of policy. So it is hardly surprising that the natural rate of unemployment has sometimes appeared to be presented as an eminently tolerable, if not actually desirable, condition. However, as the natural rate of unemployment has risen, this attitude seems to have disappeared. Everyone now agrees that something should be done to reduce the natural rate towards the desired 'full employment' level and that it will have to be something other than an expansion of aggregate demand. But the force of this agreement is limited by differences of opinion about the remaining scope for demand management.

The scope left for demand management by natural rate theory depends on the extent of labour market failure. Conviction and consensus interpretations of the natural rate share the idea that natural unemployment is an equilibrium phenomenon but exhibit deep disagreements about the time period involved. The question is whether economic agents in the labour market make price or quantity adjustments. Minford's (1985) market-clearing assumption means that in his view agents always make instantaneous price (wage) adjustments, from which it follows that the labour market is always at equilibrium. Consequently, a demand expansion would be entirely dissipated in inflation, leaving output and hence unemployment unchanged. So on this interpretation there is no scope at all for demand management. Moderate Keynesians like Layard (1986, p. 20) adopt a middle-of-the-road position, rejecting the concept of voluntary unemployment as 'fundamentally unhelpful' but conceding that unemployment is affected by, among other things, 'individual choices'. The labour market can be in disequilibrium at least for short periods. Output and unemployment take the strain of adjustment to a new policy regime because implicit or staggered contracts prevent wages from changing quickly. Implicit contracts insure workers against fluctuations in real wages, while the dates of wage contracts in different industries are frequently staggered (Davies, 1985, pp. 50–1). This means that expansionary monetary policy reduces unemployment below the natural rate in the short run.

The policy implications of the two approaches are clear. For the conviction politician, aggregate demand expansion has no role to play in so far as government policy is anticipated and therefore leads to inflation. This is what is meant by the phrase 'policy ineffectiveness'. All that is left is a set of supply-side measures such as abolishing union immunities or the closed shop and cutting unemployment benefits or making it more difficult to qualify for them. For the consensus interpretation, on the other hand, there is scope for *both* supply-side and demand-side policies. Layard for example puts forward a moderate set of policy recommendations, arguing that 'policies on aggregate demand matter. Attending to the supply side is not enough' (1986, p. 146). Similarly, according to Davies, while there is a long-run equilibrium level of employment which is not affected by demand management, 'the economy can get "stuck" in short-run "disequilibrium" states for very long periods' (1985, p. 90). So there is scope for demand management to speed the economy's return to equilibrium and reduce unemployment to the natural rate with only 'slight' inflation consequences. Equally, the acceptance of NAIRU means that attending to aggregate demand is not enough. As Knight puts it, 'it is difficult to believe that unemployment in Britain can be lowered much below two million without policies which are designed to reduce the natural rate itself' (1987, p. 268).

What about the unemployment consequences of fighting inflation by a contraction of aggregate demand? Can disinflation ever be achieved with no adverse effects on output and unemployment at all? Both the conviction and the consensus approaches hold out the happy prospect of painless disinflation but under very different conditions. These are best elucidated as competing interpretations of rational expectations theory. From a conviction perspective disinflation is painless provided only that the government unambiguously signals its commitment to defeat inflation 'whatever the consequences'. Rational economic agents will adjust their behaviour in such a way that inflation falls rapidly leaving unemployment unchanged. On the consensus interpretation, however, the government's commitment to its policy is only a necessary, not a sufficient, condition for painless disinflation. There must also be a consensus in favour of the economic model used by the government in formulating policy. These interpretations of rational expectations theory will be elaborated in Chapters 14 and 15 as the conviction and consensus approaches to macroeconomic policy making are put to the test of experience.

13.5 HYSTERESIS

It has been argued that the implication of NAIRU is that there is scope for an expansion of aggregate demand to reduce unemployment in the short run; contrary to the claims of the 'market clearers', it will not be entirely dissipated in inflation. But the behaviour of UK unemployment in the mid-1980s added to the doubts about the validity of NAIRU and prompted the emergence of an alternative theory to explain the course of unemployment and to justify active demand management.

The new perspective is based on the concept of hysteresis, according to which the equilibrium or natural rate of unemployment in the current period may depend upon the rate of unemployment in previous periods (Hargreaves Heap, 1980; Cross, 1988; Cross et al., 1988). In the mid-1980s the wage pressure factors which determine NAIRU appeared to fall, implying that NAIRU also fell. For example, the average replacement ratio dropped when the earnings-related supplement to unemployment benefit was abolished in 1982, relative import prices rose as sterling depreciated and union militancy declined under the double impact of anti-union legislation and falling membership. But while NAIRU fell actual unemployment remained high. The only way NAIRU theorists can explain this is to argue that demand deficiency unemployment (the 'non-NAIRU' component) rose because the government was pushing unemployment above NAIRU to reduce inflation. But inflation did not fall during the mid-1980s. Hysteresis does not suggest some other way of explaining the conjunction of high unemployment, stable inflation and falling NAIRU but questions the assumption that NAIRU fell.

What hysteresis does is to identify factors other than the wage push (Z) variables already incorporated into the NAIRU equation which might keep NAIRU high despite falls in the Z variables. The central idea is that even a short period of high demand deficiency unemployment might set in motion processes which increase NAIRU in subsequent years. Three main mechanisms are under investigation. First, the insider–outsider hypothesis divides labour market agents into insiders who experience uninterrupted employment and outsiders who regularly suffer spells of unemployment (Lindbeck and Snower, 1988; Blanchard and Summers, 1988). Outsiders, being perceived as less employable than insiders, have little influence on wage determination; for example they cannot 'price themselves back into jobs' by offering to work for lower wages. High unemployment creates more outsiders, effectively reducing the labour supply in subsequent years and hence raising the equilibrium rate of unemployment. Second, the long-term unemployment hypothesis holds that the skills of the long-term unemployed atrophy and their attitude to work deteriorates (Price, 1988). They look less hard for work and even when they apply for jobs tend to be turned down in favour of people with more recent work experience. Once again the effect is to reduce the supply of labour and increase the equilibrium unemployment rate. Third, the physical capital hypothesis is based on the observation that high unemployment is associated with a fall in the capital stock as investment in new capital equipment declines and existing plant is lost or destroyed as firms go out of business. The resulting fall in the ratio of capital to labour reduces the feasible real wage – each worker is worth less because he/she has less capital equipment to work with – and so NAIRU increases.

The policy implication of hysteresis is that demand management *can* influence NAIRU. A contractionary policy which causes demand deficiency unemployment also increases NAIRU in the future, while an expansionary policy secures a sustainable fall in unemployment by reducing demand deficiency unemployment now and therefore NAIRU later.

13.6 CONCLUSION

There *are* common features to the two interpretations of the natural rate of unemployment. Natural unemployment occurs when the labour market is in equilibrium; it occurs when inflation is not accelerating; it is caused by structural and institutional factors, not by demand deficiency; and it cannot be eradicated by demand expansion. But equilibrium unemployment is not the same concept as NAIRU. There is disagreement on whether the labour market is almost always in equilibrium or reaches equilibrium, if at all, only in the long run, and consequently disagreement on the emphasis to be placed on supply-side measures and the scope for demand expansion in reducing unemployment. No doubt there *is* a rate of unemployment at which the long-run Phillips curve is vertical but we do not know whether at any particular time it is closer to full employment or to the mass unemployment of the early 1980s. If all we know is that there is such a thing as natural unemployment, we know little about the severity of the inflation constraint on demand management policies to reduce unemployment. Equally, we know little about the unemployment cost of eliminating inflation. In order to find out it is necessary to examine each approach to macroeconomic policy making in the light of experience.

14. Conviction, Rational Expectations and Painless Disinflation

14.1 THE INFLATION–UNEMPLOYMENT ADJUSTMENT PATH

The conviction interpretation of the natural rate of unemployment can be elucidated by examining the idea of an inflation–unemployment adjustment path. According to Dornbusch and Fischer (1987), when an adverse supply shock increases both inflation and unemployment, 'policy makers do not choose between inflation and unemployment, but rather between *adjustment paths* that differ in the inflation–unemployment mix' (p. 573). The compromise interpretation of the natural rate underlies a gradualist disinflation policy which involves a relatively slow fall in inflation in order to minimize the increase in unemployment, while the confrontation approach informs the cold turkey strategy which seeks to eliminate inflation rapidly even at the cost of a sharp rise in unemployment (Figure 14.1). Either way, the eventual outcome is a lower inflation rate at the natural rate of unemployment, because in the long run the Phillips curve is vertical.

The disinflation of the early 1980s appears to reflect a preference among Conservative policy makers in the UK and the US for cold turkey, for buying lower inflation quickly with persistent mass unemployment. But was this outcome really intended or was it the unforeseen consequence of a policy embarked upon in the confident belief that it would eliminate inflation painlessly, without a serious unemployment cost? What did policy advisers believe about the sacrifice ratio, the rate at which unemployment had to rise to reduce inflation? The lower the sacrifice ratio, the less will be the pain of disinflation.

Figure 14.1   Inflation–unemployment adjustment paths

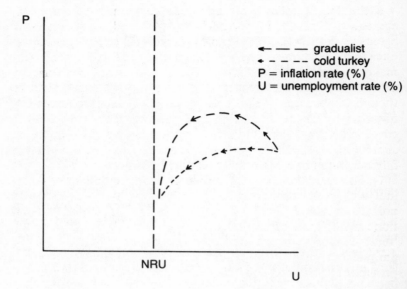

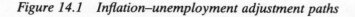

14.2   PAINLESS DISINFLATION: THE THEORY

In the extreme case the sacrifice ratio is zero; there is no
unemployment cost of reducing inflation even in the short run;
disinflation is painless. Some rational expectations theorists claim
to have identified the conditions for minimizing the sacrifice ratio
to this ultimate extent.

Expectations are rational to the extent that they are unbiased
and efficient. A prediction does not have to be correct to be
unbiased; it is enough if systematic errors are avoided. The
minimum requirement for a prediction to be efficient is that it
embody readily available information including knowledge of the
structure of the economy. The claim that policy is ineffective arises
if the argument that expectations are rational is combined with the
assumption that markets clear continuously. This means that any
change of policy will provoke an immediate adjustment to prices

in the relevant markets while quantities remain unaffected. Policy ineffectiveness can be advantageous or disadvantageous, depending on circumstances.

If the aim of policy is to reduce unemployment by increasing aggregate demand, policy ineffectiveness is bad news. Economic agents in the labour market adjust their inflation expectations at once and hence wages rise, by the amount predicted in the policy makers' model, *without delay*. There is no room for quantity adjustments and unemployment is therefore unchanged. It is as though the notional short-run Phillips curve shifts outwards immediately the policy change is announced, so that the Phillips curve is vertical at the natural rate of unemployment even in the short run. Demand expansion causes an acceleration in the inflation rate but has no effect on unemployment.

If, however, the aim is to reduce or eliminate inflation, policy ineffectiveness means that the disinflation will be painless. The point about policy ineffectiveness is that, under rational expectations and continuous market clearing, policy has no effect on the 'real' economy of quantities of goods and services. So the announcement of disinflationary fiscal or monetary policies prompts an instantaneous revision of inflationary expectations, which shifts the notional short-run Phillips curve downwards. Since this makes the operative Phillips curve vertical at the natural rate of unemployment, inflation falls at once without any increase in unemployment and the sacrifice ratio is therefore zero.

Under what conditions will disinflation be painless? Two conflicting answers are given by rational expectations theorists. From a unilateral perspective disinflation is painless provided only that the government unambiguously signals its commitment to defeat inflation 'whatever the consequences'. Rational economic agents will adjust their behaviour in such a way that inflation falls rapidly leaving unemployment unchanged. For example, Minford and Peel argue that if the government changes the money supply rule output will be unaffected because the new monetary stance is 'incorporated into people's expectations . . . and cannot cause any surprises' (1983, p. 19). Sargent, on the other hand, expounds a bilateral interpretation, according to which the government's commitment to its policy is only a necessary, not a sufficient, condition for painless disinflation. There must also be a consensus in favour of the economic model used by the government in formulating policy: 'the change in the rule for the pertinent variable must be widely understood and uncontroversial' (1986, p. 114).

It will be argued here that only under the bilateral interpretation can rational expectations contribute to a coherent theory of aggregate economic behaviour. And it will be maintained in Chapter 15 that the bilateral interpretation presupposes the consensus approach to macroeconomic policy making. The first step in the argument is to review the Thatcher government's attempt to eliminate inflation in the early 1980s.

14.3   PAINLESS DISINFLATION? THE FACTS

Matthews and Minford claim that the Thatcher government's deflationary programme 'contributed only a *small* part to the shocks which produced negative actual growth during 1980–81' (1987, p. 81). This claim rests on two main arguments. First, falling inflation raises the real value of wealth and thereby offsets the contractionary effects of tight monetary and fiscal policies on aggregate demand (Matthews, 1989, p. 108). Second, equilibrium unemployment rose sharply from 2.1 million in 1979 to 3.7 million in 1981, two-thirds of this increase being attributed to rising unionization and higher rates of income tax and unemployment benefits (ibid., p. 85). So Matthews and Minford are claiming in effect that despite appearances to the contrary the Thatcher government's disinflationary policies were painless, the pain of mass unemployment being caused by factors other than demand management policy. It will be argued here however that there was a direct and unambiguous relationship between demand management policy and unemployment during the early 1980s.

The Liverpool model understates the impact of the Thatcher government's disinflationary policies. It is hard to believe that the rapid rise in unemployment after 1979 was unrelated to the fundamental change in fiscal stance that occurred at the same time (Figure 14.2). In the graph the general government deficit, corrected for inflation and the business cycle and expressed as a percentage of GNP, is taken as a measure of the demand management policy stance. The general government deficit is preferred to the public sector borrowing requirement because it classifies asset

Figure 14.2 *Demand management and demand deficient unemployment: UK 1973–84*

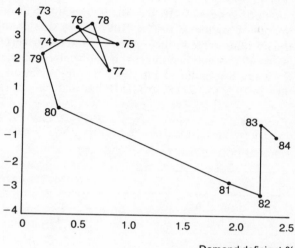

General government
deficit corrected
for inflation and
cycle as a percentage
of GNP

Demand deficient %
unemployment

sales as a means of financing the budget deficit rather than a way of reducing it. In order to measure the underlying fiscal stance, this deficit is then adjusted for changes in tax receipts and social security payments associated with cyclical variations in the level of economic activity. Since the real value or burden of the deficit is reduced by inflation and since it will be repaid from future output, the cyclically adjusted general government deficit is further corrected for inflation and economic growth.

The major change in unemployment occurred between 1979 and 1981, when it virtually doubled from 4.6 per cent to 9 per cent. At the same time, the government, as part of its anti-inflation strategy, transformed a general government deficit equal to 2.3 per cent of GNP into a general government surplus equal to 2.7 per cent of GNP. Clearly the change of policy regime in pursuit of stable prices led to the emergence of an adjusted general government surplus, which contributed to the rise in unemployment.

The years 1979–81 saw a tightening of monetary policy in terms of both nominal and real growth of narrow money (Table 14.1). Minimum lending rate rose from 9.2 per cent in 1978 to 16.2 per cent in 1980. The effect on the exchange rate and hence on the competitiveness of UK exports is difficult to disentangle from the impact of higher oil prices. But this is a side issue. An increase in the exchange rate reduces inflation and the government could have pursued alternative policies if it had wanted a lower exchange rate. So it is reasonable to interpret the appreciation of sterling from 90.9 in 1979 to 100 in 1980 (IMF multilateral exchange rate model)

Table 14.1   UK money growth 1974–79 and 1979–81

(annual percentage rates of change)

	1974–79	1979–81
Nominal M1	15.3	10.2
Real M1	−0.2	−4.1

Source: Bruno and Sachs (1985), Table 8.5.

as an instrument of monetary policy rather than an external circumstance beyond government control. In that case contractionary monetary policy was largely responsible for the decline in competitiveness which accounted for 'about half of the low aggregate demand in the early 1980s' (Layard, 1986, p. 72).

Yet Matthews and Minford insist that 'it cannot be said that deflationary domestic demand policies were a significant cause of the recession' (1987, p. 82). Their specific claim about the wealth effects of falling inflation is beside the point. Matthews argues that the contractionary effects of tight monetary and fiscal policy on aggregate demand are offset because 'the fall in the price level (inflation) raises the real value of wealth' (1989, p. 108). However, it is clear that the fall in inflation and its associated wealth effects came too late to prevent a fall in consumption in 1980 and 1981 (Table 14.2). By the time consumption started to pick up,

Table 14.2   Consumption and inflation: UK 1979–82

	Consumption £bn	Inflation rate %
1979	137.3	13.4
1980	136.8	18.0
1981	136.7	11.9
1982	138.1	8.6

Source: UK National Accounts 1984, Table 1.5; *Economic Trends Annual Supplement*, 1985, Table 4.

deflationary domestic demand policies had already had a devastating impact on economic activity, which had actually fallen in both 1980 and 1981.

The second argument used by Matthews and Minford (1987) in support of their claim that the disinflation of the early 1980s was effectively painless directly concerns the natural rate of unemployment. Equilibrium unemployment on their calculations rose from 2.1 million in 1979 to 3.7 million in 1981, mainly because of increases in trade union power and the replacement ratio. There are several grounds for scepticism about this argument.

In the first place, a rise in equilibrium unemployment means that the inflow of newly unemployed people into unemployment will be dominated by those who are voluntarily leaving their jobs. It is implicit in the expectations-augmented Phillips curve that the rise in unemployment as it returns to its natural rate occurs because people leave their jobs when they perceive the fall in their real wages. But in reality the rise in UK unemployment was accompanied by a sharp increase in redundancies from 225 000 in 1979 to 475 000 in 1981 (Figure 14.3). True, the subsequent fall in redundancies was not matched by a decline in unemployment because people remained unemployed longer. Perhaps some of those who *became* unemployed involuntarily *remained* so of their own volition. Is this the justification for Matthews and Minford's (1987) claim that it was equilibrium unemployment that rose so dramatically in the early 1980s?

Absolutely not. The Liverpool model's treatment of the replacement ratio and long-term unemployment is thoroughly implausible. Its estimate of the elasticity of unemployment with respect

Figure 14.3   Redundancies and unemployment: UK 1979–85

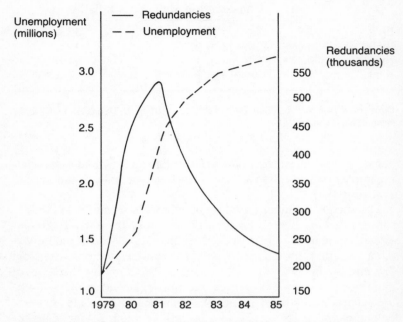

Source: Department of Employment (1986), Chart C1 and Table 2.30.

to the replacement ratio, at 2.6, is out of line with other estimates, which cluster around 0.6–0.7 (Layard and Nickell, 1985). In other words, according to the Liverpool model a specified rise in the replacement ratio increases unemployment by four times the increase estimated by other economic models. The explanation of the upward bias in the Liverpool model's elasticity estimate lies in the way in which long-term unemployment is incorporated into it.

The wage equation in that model assumes that 'the elasticity of the long-term unemployed (caught in the unemployment trap) . . . is "infinite" ' (Minford, 1985, p. 22). What this means is that, for example, an increase in the replacement ratio from 0.8 to 0.9 might lead claimants with a median unemployment duration of 20 weeks to respond 'by planning "indefinite" duration, say two years (104 weeks) to allow for an occasional sampling of work' (ibid.).

So the rise in long-term unemployment is explained in the Liverpool model as a manifestation of the unemployment trap. In this way the very high replacement ratios associated with the unemployment trap, which involves no more than about 3 per cent of the unemployed, have a disproportionate influence on the elasticity of unemployment with respect to the replacement ratio. What is worse, the unemployment trap is not a convincing explanation of the rise in long-term unemployment. The principal cause of the increase in male long-term unemployment between 1975 and 1981 was the increased inflow of skilled older workers into unemployment (Hughes and Hutchinson, 1986). *Skilled* workers are the least likely to be caught in the unemployment trap, which is largely populated by men whose lack of marketable skills limits their employment prospects to low-paid jobs. It seems clear that the Liverpool model exaggerates the importance of the replacement ratio in explaining increases in unemployment.

For all of these reasons it is impossible to be convinced by Matthews and Minford's assertion that disinflationary domestic policies were not an important influence on unemployment in the early 1980s. The question is why, when rational expectations theory held out the prospect of painless disinflation, the disinflation of that time gave rise to persistent mass unemployment. The obvious explanation is that economic agents do not as a matter of fact form their expectations of inflation rationally. They expected inflation to continue despite evidence to the contrary simply because they were not in the habit of consulting the evidence. This objection to the painless disinflation thesis is ultimately unconvincing, but a critical examination of it reveals a fundamental weakness in the unilateral interpretation of rational expectations theory.

14.4   RATIONAL EXPECTATIONS: THE 'AS IF' DEFENCE

Rational expectations theory generalizes the rationality assumption of consumer demand theory. A perfectly competitive market operates *as if* all consumers are rational, because irrational actions, being randomly distributed through a large sample, cancel out. This leaves the minority of rational agents to exert a decisive influence on aggregate behaviour. Minford and Peel define rational expectations as the belief that the typical individual 'utilizes efficiently the information available to him in forming expectations about future outcomes' (1983, p. 4). They emphasize that this is a belief about the 'typical' individual and hence 'cannot be falsified by examples of behaviour by any actual individual' (ibid., p. 5). As long as enough individuals to 'contribute a dominant proportion of the variability in aggregate behaviour' exhibit systematic rational behaviour in expectations formation, 'this would be sufficient to generate aggregate behaviour that exhibited rationality' (ibid.).

Suppose a group of workers are deciding whether or not to accept a wage settlement. The rational worker may be presumed to be seeking a target real wage rise, which he has calculated by using all available information to predict the future inflation rate. Some workers may have very different aims; they may for example wish to bring down the government, express their loyalty to an ideal of working-class solidarity or increase their differential over some other group of workers. According to rational expectations theory, the existence of these deviant intentions does not detract from the rationality of economic agents' inflationary expectations any more than impulse buying or the effects of advertising undermine the rationality assumption of consumer demand theory. Irrational actions are by definition randomly distributed through the population. Therefore, given a sufficiently large sample, intentions to pursue wage settlements in excess of the target will be cancelled out by intentions to accept something less, perhaps out of a sense of duty to patients or pupils or an unwillingness to accept the financial penalty of strike action. The outcome is *as if* each economic agent formulated a target rise in real wages based on an unbiased and efficient prediction of inflation.

So the objection made for example by Hillier (1986) that economic agents do not form expectations rationally is beside the point. According to Hillier, 'it is still possible to argue that the man or woman in the street simply does not form rational expectations' (1986, p. 169), because 'in the real world' it is too costly to acquire and process information. Admitting that the line of defence for rational expectations appears to be that it is 'an abstraction to be judged not by its realism but by its effects on the performance of empirical models' (ibid.), Hillier nevertheless concludes that the actual procedure individuals use to form expectations is a matter for empirical as well as theoretical research and that adaptive expectations may be more plausible in certain circumstances (ibid., p. 170).

This sort of objection is misguided in focusing on the behaviour of actual individuals, which is irrelevant because rational expectations theory does not assume that all or even most individuals form expectations rationally. What it *does* assume is that (a) some individuals form expectations rationally, and (b) those who do not form expectations rationally do not form them in any systematic way at all. The second part of the assumption is crucial because it is the random distribution of irrational expectations that allows aggregate behaviour to exhibit rationality. Irrationally high inflation forecasts roughly cancel out irrationally low inflation forecasts and so it is the rationally formulated expectations that exert the decisive influence on aggregate behaviour. So the 'as if' defence of rational expectations theory holds good against the obvious objection. But the 'as if' defence makes an assumption that will eventually destroy the unilateral interpretation of rational expectations theory and with it the conviction approach to macro-economic policy making.

14.5 RATIONAL EXPECTATIONS, AGGREGATE BEHAVIOUR AND IDEOLOGY

Disinflation can in principle be painless if, although not only if, expectations are formed rationally. The 'as if' defence of rational expectations theory is proof against the standard objection that it has no empirical foundations. That defence relies on the random nature of subjective departures from rationality by individuals, which means that aggregate inflationary expectations are unbiased. It is vulnerable to the argument to be advanced here that in the labour market departures from rationality are likely to be ideologically inspired and hence systematic. In that case inflationary expectations are likely to be biased and disinflation to be painful.

The fundamental assumption of the 'as if' defence is that labour market operators can fail to be rational only by succumbing to subjective, randomly distributed feelings. This assumption is a weakness that undermines the entire unilateral interpretation of rational expectations theory. The essential point is that it is paradoxical to rely on an assumption about the rationality of individual behaviour in trying to understand the effects of *collective* bargaining. Labour markets tend to be characterized by the existence of contracts, not between trade unions and firms, but between trade unions and workers. This is particularly true of the UK, where approximately 50 per cent of workers belong to trade unions, compared to a unionization rate of only about 12 per cent in the US. The consequence of the existence of contracts between trade unions and workers is that the subjective preferences of individual consumers find no counterpart in the labour market. A particular deviant intention may be held by the representatives of a significant proportion of workers. Departures from the norm of utility-maximizing rationality may systematically distort the outcome instead of being lost in the law of averages.

Is there any reason to believe that the expectations of labour market agents are likely to be systematically distorted? In some circumstances people believe the propositions they *want* to believe irrespective of the evidence for or against them. This 'cognitive dissonance' (Akerlof, 1984) does not in itself damage the rational expectations assumption, because such irrational attitudes might be randomly dispersed among the population according to individual psychology. However, within the general category of irrationally held beliefs there are ideological beliefs which can be systematically linked to membership of social groups. If a particular belief seems to further the interests of a social group, the members of that group may accept it without serious consideration of the relevant evidence or even despite the existence of evidence to the contrary. This is compatible with aggregate behaviour that exhibits rationality only if the social groups involved are small, numerous and have different interests. In so far as social classes or trade unions influence the formation of expectations by individuals, irrational expectations will not 'cancel out'. Aggregate behaviour will therefore be systematically distorted. Unlike the standard 'unrealistic' objection to rational expectations, the 'ideology objection' is *not* beside the point. The implication is that aggregate behaviour in the labour market will *not* be 'as if' the typical individual made efficient use of the available information to arrive at an unbiased prediction of inflation.

The policy implication is clear: if inflationary expectations are ideologically, and hence systematically, distorted, policy *can* be effective. Expansionary monetary and fiscal policies *can* cut unemployment, and disinflation will be far from painless. The claim that policy is powerless to affect the real economy is based on the assumption 'that in some aggregate sense expectations are unbiased. Even if expectations are inefficient and vary greatly around the true value, there is no basis for effective policy unless the errors are systematic, that is the expectations are biased' (Carter and Maddock, 1984, pp. 141–2). If expectations are formed ideologically so that they reflect the desires or interests of a small number of large social groups, they will be biased and there will be a basis for effective policy. If the policy objective is to reduce or eliminate inflation, this means that the disinflation is likely to have significant output and unemployment costs.

14.6 CONCLUSION

The conviction approach to macroeconomic policy making, embodying the unilateral interpretation of rational expectations theory, promises painless disinflation provided only that policy makers signal the change of policy regime unambiguously and emphatically. However the disinflation in the UK of the early 1980s was anything but painless and attempts to blame the recession on factors other than contractionary monetary and fiscal policies are unconvincing. The explanation lies in the unrealistic assumptions of the underlying theory. Clear signals of the policy change are not enough; it is not enough for the government to have the courage of its own convictions. Unless economic agents share the main objectives of macroeconomic policy, their expectations of the future course of the economy will not be unbiased or rational and their actions will frustrate the government's policy measures. The implication is that governments can minimize the costs of disinflation by building a consensus in favour of the policy objective, the approach to be tested against experience in the next chapter.

15. Consensus

15.1 INTRODUCTION

It was argued in Chapter 14 that disinflation in the UK in the early 1980s was far from painless despite the promise of some rational expectations theorists that it could be. The implication is that the conviction approach, embodying the unilateral interpretation of rational expectations theory, is wrong about the conditions required for disinflation to be painless. And that interpretation was indeed found to be based upon the unconvincing assumption that expectations can fail to be rational only through subjective, random errors committed by individuals thinking for themselves. Against this it was suggested that policy can be effective and hence disinflation painful if expectations are systematically, perhaps ideologically, distorted. The aim of this chapter is to explore this idea by using it in the development of the consensus approach to macroeconomic policy making.

The consensus interpretation of rational expectations theory recognizes the probability that inflationary expectations appear to be systematically distorted. But this *is* only an appearance and it will be argued that economic agents do more than merely predict government policies in an effort to forecast inflation and alter their behaviour accordingly. They also set out to resist and even to change policies. This means that policies can be effective only if economic agents are willing to change their behaviour in the way required for the policy to work. For example, disinflation will be painless only if agents share the goal of price stability or at least lower inflation. So the conditions for painless disinflation include agreement on policy objectives between government and economic agents.

Once the consensus approach has been expounded it will be tested against the empirical evidence in the form of a survey of the unemployment cost of disinflation in large OECD economies. The purpose of this exercise is to discover whether disinflation is less

176

painful in economies where macroeconomic policy making is based on consensus than in economies where the confrontation approach rules.

15.2 FROM THE MARKET TO THE POWER STRUGGLE

It became clear towards the end of the last chapter that disinflation will involve output and unemployment costs if expectations are ideologically distorted and hence biased. In reply confrontationists might use the 'damp squib' gambit: it is a valid point in itself but it does not do any serious damage to their interpretation of rational expectations theory. If trade unions are the only source of *systematic* bias in expectations formation in the labour market, it is only *their* expectations that have to be unbiased for expectations to be rational. As long as trade unions rely on expert inflation forecasts and all other individuals in the labour market either follow their lead or play their own subjective hunches, the outcome will indeed be as if all individuals made efficient use of the available information to formulate an unbiased prediction of inflation. So policy will be effective and disinflation painless to the extent that unbiased expert forecasts are incorporated into trade union behaviour.

It is important to see how restricted is the conception of rationality implicit in the confrontation interpretation of rational expectations theory. It is as if its adherents, being professionally involved in making disinterested predictions about economic variables, assume that this is what *all* economic agents are trying to do. If that were true, they would not be *agents* at all but 'rational fools'. For this understanding of rational expectations theory implies that agents perceive their interests but act in a way that frustrates them. And that is irrational.

The fundamental fault in the confrontation approach is the assumption that the only reason that agents' aggregate behaviour could be inconsistent with policy is that they have got it wrong. Of course the argument is that, being rational, agents do not get it wrong. They form expectations rationally and adjust their price and wage behaviour immediately. So policy leaves everything in the real economy as it was and disinflation is painless. But perhaps agents do not form expectations with the sole aim of adjusting their behaviour to them. Perhaps their aim is to influence rather than merely forecast the future course of economic events.

Consider the early years of Mrs Thatcher's first administration. From the confrontation perspective, unemployment rose because trade unions misjudged the government's determination to pursue disinflationary polices. Wage claims appeared to embody a higher inflation forecast than was warranted in the light of policy statements. If expectations are rational, this could have happened only because the government failed to convince labour market agents that there would be no U-turn. As long as policy makers send the right signals, rational agents will adjust their behaviour in such a way that policy reduces inflation without increasing unemployment. The problem with this model of economic behaviour is that it assumes that all economic agents, including the government, possess common interests and goals.

This assumption is challenged by partisan theories of macroeconomic policy, which argue that governments pursue policies which redistribute income towards their supporters (Alesina, 1989). According to Hibbs (1987), an increase in US unemployment is associated with a fall in the incomes shares of the two poorest quintiles and a rise in the shares of the two richest quintiles. Minford (1985) argues that inflation has the opposite effect by eroding the real value of nominally denominated assets which are most likely to be held by the upper middle class. So the first priority of left-wing governments is to seek to cut unemployment, while right-wing governments are mainly concerned to reduce inflation. A disinflationary policy put forward by a right-wing government is likely to be perceived as ideological in the pejorative sense that it seeks to sustain a putatively unjust or exploitative distribution of income (Geuss, 1981, pp. 12–22).

The implication of this line of thought is that even if the Thatcher government's commitment to its disinflationary monetary and fiscal policies had been beyond doubt private agents might still have behaved *as if* they were unsure of its resolve. If trade union members believed that disinflation would adversely affect their collective interests, they had a reason for acting as if they expected inflation to continue unabated. For they might have caused the downfall of a policy which they perceived to be against their interests. Rational agents will act as if they expect inflation to fall only if they share the government's desire that it should do so.

It is true that disinflation will be painless to the extent that unbiased expert forecasts are incorporated into trade union behaviour. In a world of rational economic agents, collective interests and partisan governments, the partisan nature of policy making will be perceived by trade unions and used in the formation not so much of expectations as of policies. The distinction between policy makers and other economic agents effectively collapses. If working-class representatives who are aware of the conditions for painless disinflation believe that inflation increases the share of wages in national income at the expense of profits, they have a reason for acting as if they expected the current rate of inflation to continue. In the right circumstances such behaviour will induce a rise in unemployment sufficient to cause a reversal of the disinflationary policies. It is therefore reasonable to interpret trade union policy as if it were the outcome of a systematic attempt by members to weigh the benefits of reversing disinflation by increasing the share of wages in national income against the costs of reversing disinflation by incurring the adverse redistributive effects of higher unemployment.

Real wage rigidity is best understood as a form of policy resistance rather than as the product of a misjudgement of the strength of the government's determination to defeat inflation. In so far as wage push inflation is a trade union policy instrument for securing a redistribution of national income, disinflationary policies will encounter opposition rather than incredulity. UK inflation in the 1970s appears to have increased the share of wages in national income at the expense of profits (Brown, 1985, pp. 273–4). So trade unions could reasonably see the Thatcher government's disinflationary policies as a partisan attempt to restore the share of profits in national income.

The conviction politician's picture of economic behaviour commits economic agents to irrationality. The phenomenon to be explained is a power struggle, a conflict over the distribution of national income, not a failure to make efficient use of available information in the formation of inflationary expectations. An efficient and unbiased prediction of inflation entails that on unchanged policies the share of wages in national income is going to decline. Rational trade unions must therefore be presumed to

know that adjusting their behaviour in line with 'rational expectations' will be inimical to the interests of their members. So, acting
on the basis of rational expectations is irrational. The rational
course of action is to act as if inflationary expectations were
formed adaptively or even extrapolatively, unless there are
grounds for believing that the costs of reversing disinflationary
policies outweigh the benefits. Only the consensus interpretation
of rational expectations theory recognizes the fact that economic
agents might be trying to change the future course of inflation
rather than adjust their behaviour in the light of inflationary
expectations.

The consensus version of rational expectations indicates the
conditions, if not for painless, then at least for 'low cost', disinflation. The theory predicts that the sacrifice ratio will be lower
to the degree that expectations are either unbiased or biased in
favour of the disinflationary policies in force. The question is
whether sacrifice ratios are lower in economies where policy
making is informed by the consensus approach.

15.3   CORPORATISM AND MACROECONOMIC PERFORMANCE

The central contention of the consensus interpretation is that the
cost of disinflation depends on the extent to which the policy
objective is shared by economic agents. In order to test this
hypothesis it is helpful to distinguish between corporatist and non-
corporatist economies and to examine their relative macroeconomic performance. Corporatist economies are characterized
by a high degree of consensus on macroeconomic policy objectives. Soskice (1983) identifies shared perspectives between labour
and firms on the goals of economic activity as a central feature of
corporatism. Bruno and Sachs identify Sweden as 'an outstanding
example' of corporatism on the basis of factors which include 'a
high degree of social consensus concerning the norms of wage
bargains' (1985, p. 224), indicated by low levels of strike activity.
The other factors reflect the conditions under which consensus is
most likely to evolve: a high degree of unionization; highly
centralized wage bargaining; national agreements as the basis of
wage setting in the whole economy; and high levels of government

participation in the economy. The macroeconomic performance of corporatist and non-corporatist economies has been compared in a number of different ways with the results consistently favouring the corporatist economies.

Bruno and Sachs (1985) relate a corporatism index to a misery index. The corporatism index reflects the degree of union centralization, the extent of shop-floor union power, employer co-ordination and the presence of works councils; the misery index measures the rise in inflation plus the slowdown in real GNP growth after 1973 (1985, p. 227). They find a strong negative correlation ($r = -0.68$), meaning that corporatism is associated with a superior record on inflation and economic growth. Soskice (1983) reports a similar conclusion from an OECD investigation, which found an inverse association between the degree of consensus and the Okun misery index defined as the sum of inflation and unemployment rates. Another indicator of macroeconomic performance favoured by Bruno and Sachs is the trade-off between inflation and output. They estimate that 'on average, a 1 percentage point rise in GNP growth during 1973–79 is associated with a 1.4 percentage point rise in inflation between 1973 and 1979' and that corporatist economies 'do significantly better than average in this trade-off' (1985, p. 229).

Newell and Symons (1986) found that the effect on unemployment of a wage shock such as an increase in trade union militancy or an employment shock such as a rise in real interest rates was greater in non-corporatist economies and in the non-corporatist phases of economies whose degree of corporatism had changed over time. For example, the unemployment consequences of such shocks were six times greater in non-corporatist post-1979 UK than in corporatist pre-1979 UK. Corporatist economies also needed a smaller increase in unemployment to cut real wages (Table 15.1). So a number of inquiries using different methods reach the conclusion that corporatist economies perform better than non-corporatist ones.

However, to indicate in general terms the superior macro-economic performance of corporatist economies is not to establish beyond reasonable doubt that the disinflation of the early 1980s was less painful in such economies. The fact that corporate outperform non-corporatist economies in terms of the misery index, the unemployment consequences of wage and employment

Table 15.1   The impact of unemployment on real wages

	Percentage point fall in real wages in response to a 1% rise in unemployment
Corporatist	
Sweden	3.28
West Germany pre-1977	1.53
UK pre-1979	1.90
Japan pre-1977	5.61
Non-corporatist	
West Germany post-1977	0.38
UK post-1979	0.14
Japan post-1977	1.82
USA	0.19

Source: Metcalf (1987), Table 3, p. 60.

shocks and the output–inflation trade-off suggests that they also have lower sacrifice ratios.

15.4   CORPORATISM AND SACRIFICE RATIOS

The question is whether corporatist economies disinflate at lower sacrifice ratios than non-corporatist ones, *ceteris paribus*. In order to answer this it is necessary to devise a valid method of measuring the sacrifice ratio and identify any factors disturbing the *ceteris paribus* clause whose influence it is reasonable to exclude.

A crude method of measuring the sacrifice ratio is to define it as the slope of the Phillips curve and calculate it according to the formula

SR = fall in inflation 1980–83/rise in unemployment 1980–83.

But this approach does not allow meaningful comparisons of sacrifice ratios. There are two problems: inflation did not peak in the same year in all economies, and the duration of the disinflation varied across economies. The first problem can be solved by measuring the fall in inflation for each economy from its peak in 1980, 1981 or 1982 to the lowest rate achieved, usually about 3 per cent, by 1986 at the latest. As for the second problem, the solution is to calculate the 'sacrifice' as the *cumulative* increase in unemployment during those years. The sacrifice ratio should be measured according to the formula

SR = cumulative rise in unemployment/fall in inflation.

The cumulative sacrifice ratios for the major OECD economies during the disinflation of the early 1980s are shown in Table 15.2 and Figure 15.1

The second problem is to make the *ceteris paribus* clause operative, or in other words to ensure that other things *were* equal. In practice this means that the influence of the inflation rate with

Table 15.2   Sacrifice ratios in the disinflation of the early 1980s

	Inflation %			Cumulative increase in unemployment % points	Sacrifice ratio
	Peak/year	Low/year	Fall A–B		
	A	B	C	D	E
Austria	6.3 81	3.0 85	3.3	17.0	5.15
W. Germany	4.8 80	3.3 83	1.5	22.8	15.20
Netherlands	5.7 80	1.9 83	3.8	37.7	9.92
Norway	14.6 80	5.2 85	9.4	15.3	1.63
Sweden	11.7 80	6.7 85	5.0	17.2	3.44
Denmark	10.6 82	4.9 86	5.7	43.7	7.66
Switzerland	6.9 81	3.3 83	4.2	3.5	0.81
Finland	11.7 81	3.5 86	8.2	31.0	3.78
Japan	3.8 80	3.2 81	0.6	4.2	7.00
Belgium	7.1 82	3.7 86	3.4	60.9	17.91
Italy	20.6 80	8.0 86	12.6	63.9	5.07
France	11.7 82	4.7 86	7.0	46.7	6.67
UK	19.7 80	3.5 86	16.2	70.5	4.35
USA	9.5 81	3.4 83	6.1	26.5	4.34

Source: OECD (1988), Tables 8.1 (columns A and B) and 2.15 (column D).

Figure 15.1   Corporatism and the sacrifice ratio

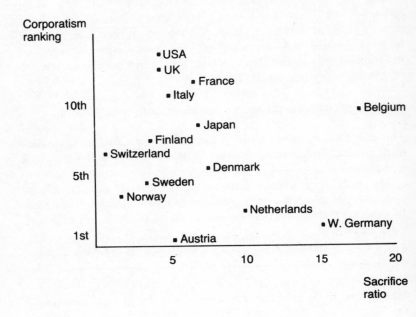

which an economy entered the 1980s must be discounted. The reason is simple. With the exception of Norway, non-corporatist economies tended to enter the 1980s with higher inflation than corporatist economies (Table 15.2, column A). If disinflation is interpreted as a downward or south-easterly move along the stylized short-run Phillips curve which becomes gradually flatter as the rate of inflation declines, high inflation economies can be expected to exhibit lower sacrifice ratios. This effect masks the influence of corporatism on the sacrifice ratio. For example, the effect of West Germany's high corporatism ranking is overridden by its very low inflation rate. Since the relatively low initial inflation rates characteristic of many corporatist economies reflect their superior macroeconomic performance, it is appropriate to try to exclude their influence on sacrifice ratios. The cumulative sacrifice ratios of high inflation OECD economies are shown in Table 15.3.

Table 15.3 *Sacrifice ratios in high inflation OECD economies by degree of corporatism*

	Corporatism ranking	Peak inflation rate	Sacrifice ratio
Corporatist high inflation			
Norway	4	14.6	1.63:1
Sweden	5	11.7	3.44:1
Non-corporatist high inflation			
Italy	11	20.6	5.07:1
UK	13	19.7	4.35:1
France	12	11.7	6.67:1

Source: As Table 15.2.

The cumulative unemployment cost of disinflating from a relatively high initial annual inflation rate to a rate of or approaching 3 per cent *does* vary according to the corporatism rankings (Tables 15.2, column D, and 15.3 and Figure 15.2). That is to say, corporatist high inflation economies exhibit lower cumulative sacrifice ratios than non-corporatist high inflation economies (Table 15.3). The figures show that in the early 1980s economies disinflating from a position of double-digit inflation achieved sacrifice ratios of between 1:1 and 7:1. If the economy was clearly corporatist, the sacrifice ratio was within the range 1:1 to 4:1, while a paradigmatically non-corporatist economy exhibited a sacrifice ratio between 4:1 and 7:1. Clearly, the cumulative unemployment cost of disinflation in high inflation economies is lower if policy making and institutions are corporatist.

There is more here than a set of unexplained correlations. Metcalf qualifies his endorsement of the empirical research by claiming that 'the *performance–consensus–corporatism* nexus does not, however, identify the causal mechanism' (1987, p. 59). But the empirical data have been used here precisely as a test of a putative causal mechanism, derived from the consensus interpretation of rational expectations theory. The hypothesis is that the cost of disinflation will be lower to the extent that expectations are unbiased, that is to the extent that economic agents behave *as if* they were using the same economic model as the government.

*Figure 15.2   Corporatism and the unemployment cost of
disinflation*

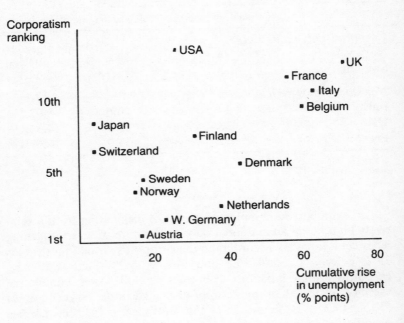

Under a corporatist regime, most economic agents actually do share policy makers' beliefs about the structure and working of the economy and their objectives. Corporatism puts in place the conditions required for rational expectations formation, once it is realized that they include not only unambiguous signals from the government but also a consensus among economic agents on the objectives and principles of policy. The consensus interpretation yields a prediction which experience fails to falsify.

15.5   CONCLUSION

For relatively high inflation economies, where disinflation is most likely to be the optimal strategy, the unemployment cost of reducing the rate of inflation is likely to be lower in corporatist economies where economic agents share a common model of the economy and a common set of policy objectives.

It seems to be the case that, whatever the degree of corporatism, disinflation from an initial inflation rate of 10 per cent or less is likely to be achieved only at an above-average unemployment cost, perhaps on a sacrifice ratio as high as 10:1 or even higher. Non-corporatist economies disinflating from an initial inflation rate of 10–20 per cent will probably face a substantial unemployment cost, probably exhibiting sacrifice ratios in the range 4:1–7:1.

Corporatist economies in the same situation can expect to reduce inflation at a lower unemployment cost, on a sacrifice ratio of less than 4:1.

16. Deflating the Dogma of Conservative Economics

16.1 INTRODUCTION

The principal polemical aim of this book has been to establish that there is no foundation in economic theory and evidence for the Conservative dogma that inflation is the root of all economic evil and price stability the key to growth and full employment. It was argued in Chapter 12 that there is no inexorable process which converts creeping inflation ultimately into hyperinflation and by which the ever-accelerating inflation causes unemployment. The assumption that inflation causes unemployment and must be eliminated before full employment can be achieved has become the new orthodoxy in macroeconomic policy analysis. So the logical consequence of rejecting this is a return to the older orthodoxy of the trade-off between inflation and unemployment. In that context it is necessary to quantify the costs of unemployment and the costs of inflation in order to ascertain which is the more damaging and to discover the optimal combination of inflation and unemployment. The purpose of this chapter is to review the findings of Part II about the costs of unemployment and inflation and of Part III about the terms of the trade-off between them.

16.2 THE OPTIMAL COMBINATION OF UNEMPLOYMENT AND INFLATION

Were policy makers in the UK and the US right to tolerate a rise in unemployment in order to reduce the rate of inflation? Did their disinflationary policies move them nearer to or further away from the optimal combination of unemployment and inflation? But, first, what is meant by the optimal combination of unemployment and inflation? Orthodox economic theory implies that it is the combination of unemployment and inflation which equates the rate at which society is willing to exchange higher unemployment for lower inflation and the rate at which unemployment must increase in order to bring about a specified fall in inflation. What is needed is a theoretical framework for identifying the optimal or welfare-maximizing combination of inflation and unemployment.

The relevant piece of economic theory is simply a 'macro' version of indifference curve analysis. The available combinations of unemployment and inflation are plotted along the Phillips Curve PC^0, which is equivalent to the budget line of consumer demand theory (Figure 16.1). If, for example, the government's objective is a particular rate of unemployment, economists can use PC^0 to discover the rate of inflation it will have to tolerate. Of course in this macro context it is possible combinations of misery-

Figure 16.1   *The optimal combination of unemployment and inflation*

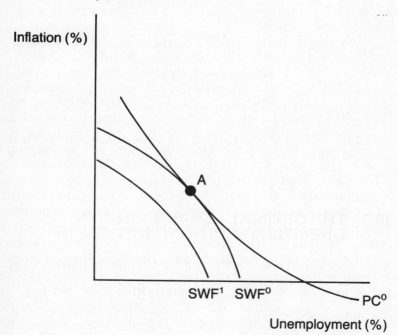

inducing 'bads' (inflation and unemployment) rather than utility-conferring goods that matter.

The next stage is to represent society's preferences between different combinations of unemployment and inflation. The social welfare function SWF^0 plots all the combinations of inflation and unemployment which yield the same amount of *dis*utility or misery to society as a whole. If, for example, 10 per cent inflation and 2 per cent unemployment leaves society approximately as well off as, say, 5 per cent inflation and 4 per cent unemployment, both combinations would lie on the same SWF. Society would be better off with 5 per cent inflation and 2 per cent unemployment and so this combination would be located on a SWF nearer to the origin, such as SWF^1.

It is now possible to identify the optimal combination of unemployment and inflation, that is, the available combination which maximizes social welfare (by minimizing misery). Combinations along SWF^1 are preferable to those along SWF^0 but none of them is also on PC^0. The combination represented by point A, where SWF^0 is tangential to PC^0, is the most desirable of the available combinations.

To say that at point A SWF^0 is tangential to PC^0 means, of course, that at that point the slope of the two curves is identical. The slope of the Phillips curve measures the rate at which unemployment can be 'exchanged' for inflation. When unemployment is low, any further increase in the demand for labour will cause a sharp rise in wage, and hence price, inflation, as firms bid up wages in an effort to attract workers. So a small fall in unemployment will be accompanied by a large rise in inflation, shown by the steep slope of the Phillips curve near the vertical axis. When unemployment is high, workers are unwilling to accept job offers below the prevailing wage rate. Consequently, wage rates fall only slowly and the slope of the Phillips curve is shallow near the horizontal axis (Phillips, 1958, p. 238). In empirical terms, the slope of the Phillips curve, or the rate at which unemployment can be traded off against inflation, is measured by the sacrifice ratio.

The slope of the social welfare function measures the rate at which society is willing to exchange more unemployment for less inflation, or less unemployment for more inflation. This is the marginal rate of substitution of inflation for unemployment. The fact that this social welfare function is concave to the origin, when indifference curves are convex, is easily explained. SWF^0 plots points of equal misery, not points of equal utility. When unemployment is low and inflation high, society is willing to trade off a relatively large rise in unemployment to secure a relatively small fall in inflation. So the slope of SWF^0 is shallow near the vertical axis. When unemployment is high and inflation low, society is prepared to tolerate a sharp rise in inflation in exchange for a small cut in unemployment. So the slope of SWF^0 is steep near the horizontal axis.

16.3   THE PHILLIPS CURVE AND THE SACRIFICE RATIO

The sacrifice ratio is the increase in unemployment needed to bring about a specified fall in the inflation rate. The cumulative sacrifice ratios for the major OECD economies during the disinflation of the early 1980s were estimated in Chapter 15, using the formula SR = cumulative rise in unemployment/fall in inflation. The fall in inflation is measured from the year in which inflation peaked in each economy to the year in which the lowest rate, usually about 3 per cent, was achieved. Only the cumulative increase in unemployment during those years measures the sacrifice of lost jobs and output, the pain of disinflation.

The results were clear. No low inflation economies, whether corporatist or non-corporatist, achieved a low sacrifice ratio. Among high inflation economies, the sacrifice ratio was lower in corporatist ones, at less than 4:1 against 4:1–7:1. For the UK and the US the results were remarkably similar. In the UK reducing inflation by 16 percentage points required a cumulative increase in unemployment of 70.5 percentage points, putting the sacrifice ratio at 4.35:1, while in the US a cumulative increase in unemployment of 26.5 percentage points was needed to cut 6.1 percentage points off inflation for a sacrifice ratio of 4.34:1. A sufficiently precise figure to work with is 4:1 for both economies, meaning that the cost of 1 percentage point of disinflation is 4 percentage points of unemployment.

Is it worth paying 4 percentage points on the unemployment rate in order to buy a fall of 1 percentage point in the inflation rate?

Suppose that inflation does four times as much economic and social damage as unemployment. A fall of 1 percentage point in the inflation rate would increase social welfare by the same amount as the accompanying rise in unemployment of 4 percentage points would reduce it. Society would be indifferent between the old and the new combinations of unemployment and inflation. If, however, unemployment does the same amount of damage as inflation, percentage point for percentage point, then trading off 4 percentage points more unemployment for 1 percentage point less inflation would reduce social welfare. The suboptimality of disinflation is even clearer if the costs of an extra percentage point on the rate of unemployment are greater than the costs of an extra percentage point of inflation (and hence greater than the benefits of a percentage point of disinflation). So the macroeconomic transaction undertaken by the governments of the UK and the US, buying each percentage point less inflation at a cost of 4 percentage points more unemployment, was worth while only if inflation is at least four times as damaging to social welfare as unemployment.

16.4   THE SLOPE OF THE SOCIAL WELFARE FUNCTION

The slope of the social welfare function (see Figure 16.1) is determined by the relative costs of unemployment and inflation. It represents society's willingness to trade off unemployment against inflation, and the terms of the trade-off reflect people's perceptions of the misery caused by each of the two phenomena. In order to plot the social welfare function in the empirical terms relevant to the disinflation of the early 1980s, all that has to be done is to review the estimates of the costs of unemployment and the costs of inflation from Part II. The benchmark is that social welfare will be unchanged if, given that it takes 4 percentage points of unemployment to reduce inflation by 1 percentage point, the costs of inflation are four times as high as the costs of unemployment.

With that benchmark in mind, three possible outcomes may be distinguished. First, if the costs of 1 percentage point of inflation are very much more than four times greater than the costs of 1 percentage point of unemployment, disinflation would be the optimal policy. Second, if 1 percentage point of unemployment is more damaging than 1 percentage point of inflation, even if only marginally, disinflation may be decisively rejected. In fact social welfare would be increased by reflating the economy, tolerating higher inflation in order to bring unemployment down. Third, if the result is close to the benchmark, if inflation is about four times more damaging than unemployment, percentage point for percentage point, the economy is already close to the social welfare maximizing equilibrium at point A (Figure 16.1), so the policy recommendation is to do nothing that might upset that position.

How do the costs of unemployment and inflation compare? The standard indicator of the level of social welfare is the level of gross national product, so the question is in effect how the *output* costs of unemployment and inflation compare. But it is worth remembering that this ignores the human costs of unemployment, because they are not measurable in monetary terms, and the redistributive effects of unemployment (which were found to be more serious than those of moderate inflation), because they leave the level of GNP unchanged. The consequence of relying on output loss is that some of the damage done by unemployment is unrecorded.

The output costs of unemployment and inflation may now be compared. For the UK an unemployment rate of 11 per cent in 1983 was associated with output loss of 11–12 per cent, perhaps even 14 per cent, of GDP, while for the US in the same year 9 per cent unemployment was accompanied by output loss of 7 per cent of GNP (Chapter 7). So 1 percentage point on the unemployment rate is likely to cut national output by approximately 1 percentage point, perhaps a little more than that in the UK, perhaps a little less in the US. In the light of the 4:1 benchmark, the question now is whether 1 percentage point on the inflation rate causes more than 4 per cent of national output to be lost. The answer is a resounding no. The shoe leather costs of 1 percentage point of moderate inflation are no more than 0.1 per cent of GDP for the UK and 0.2 per cent of GNP for the US (Chapter 11). The output loss caused by the menu costs of 1 percentage point of moderate inflation is even less significant, at 0.008 per cent of GDP for the UK. The international competitiveness and inflationary noise arguments were rejected on theoretical and empirical grounds. Far from being the more costly malfunction of the economic system, inflation causes only a fraction of the damage inflicted by unemployment.

16.5 CONCLUSION

The disinflation of the early 1980s massively reduced social well-being. Why? First, moderate inflation does not in normal circumstances accelerate into hyperinflation and it does not cause unemployment. Second, the increase in unemployment largely caused by disinflationary policies was greater than anticipated; painless disinflation proved to be a chimera. Third, the costs of unemployment are greater than those of moderate inflation and in particular the output loss is much greater. It is extraordinary that the entire direction of macroeconomic policy was changed because of a fear of inflation wholly unsupported by quantitative evidence of the damage it does. All those computers, all those econometric models, all those algebraic formulae, all those official statistics – and none of them can explain why inflation is such a terrible thing that it is worth sacrificing millions of jobs to eradicate it.

By the middle of 1991 Conservative macroeconomic policy makers in the US had softened their disinflationary stance so far as to urge interest rate cuts and acknowledge the merits of low inflationary growth rather than non-inflationary growth. But in the UK such calls were dismissed as the 'siren voices' of electoral calculation. The Prime Minister banished any thoughts of painless disinflation by insisting that 'if it isn't hurting, it isn't working'. The Chancellor of the Exchequer trumpeted a record rise in unemployment as a price 'well worth paying' to defeat inflation, refusing to learn the one indisputable lesson of the monetarist experiment – it should never be repeated.

References

Akerlof, G. (1984), *An Economic Theorist's Book of Tales*, Cambridge: Cambridge University Press.

Alesina, A. (1989), 'Politics and business cycles in industrial democracies', *Economic Policy*, **8**, April, 55–98.

Artis, M.J. (ed.) (1986), *The UK Economy: A Manual of Applied Economics*, London: Weidenfeld & Nicolson.

Atkinson, A.B. (1985), *Income Maintenance and Social Security: A Survey*, Suntory-Toyota International Centre for Economics and Related Disciplines, London School of Economics, Discussion Paper No. 5, November.

Bank of England (1984), *Quarterly Bulletin*, June.

Baumol, W.J. and Blinder, A.S. (1988), *Economics: Principles and Policy*, New York: Harcourt Brace Jovanovich.

Begg, D.K.H. (1982), *The Rational Expectations Revolution in Macroeconomics*, Oxford: Philip Allan.

Begg, D.K.H., Fischer, S. and Dornbusch, R. (1991), *Economics*, London and New York: McGraw-Hill.

Black, J. (1985), *The Economics of Modern Britain*, Oxford: Basil Blackwell.

Blanchard, O.J. and Summers, L.H. (1988), 'Hysteresis and the European Unemployment Problem', in Cross (1988).

Bootle, R. (1981), 'How important is it to defeat inflation? – The evidence', *Three Banks Review*, **132**, 23–47.

Brenner, M.H. (1977), 'Health costs and benefits of economic policy', *International Journal of Health Services*, **1**, 581–623.

Brenner, M.H. (1979), 'Mortality and the national economy: a review, and the experience of England and Wales, 1936–76', *The Lancet*, 15 September, 568–73.

Brown, A.J. (1985), *World Inflation Since 1950*, Cambridge: Cambridge University Press.

Brown, C.V. (1984), *Unemployment and Inflation*, Oxford: Basil Blackwell.

Brown, W. (1976), 'Incomes policy and pay differentials', *Oxford Bulletin of Economics and Statistics*, **38**, 27–51.

Bruno, M. and Sachs, J. (1985), *Economics of Worldwide Stagflation*, Cambridge, MA: Harvard University Press.

Carr-Hill, R.A. and Stern, N.H. (1983), 'Unemployment and crime: a comment', *Journal of Social Policy*, **12**, (3), 391–4.

Carter, M. and Maddock, R. (1984), *Rational Expectations: Macroeconomics for the 1980s?*, London: Macmillan.

Central Statistical Office (1984), *United Kingdom National Accounts*, 1984 Edition, London: HMSO.

Central Statistical Office (1985), *Economic Trends*, 1985 Edition, London: HMSO.

Central Statistical Office (1985), *Economic Trends Annual Supplement*, 1985 Edition, London: HMSO.

Clark, A. and Layard, R. (1989), *UK Unemployment*, Oxford: Heinemann Educational.

Coddington, A. (1983), *Keynesian Economics: The Search for First Principles*, London: George Allen and Unwin.

Cross, R. (ed.) (1988), *Unemployment, Hysteresis and the Natural Rate Hypothesis*, Oxford: Basil Blackwell.

Cross, R., Hutchinson, H. and Yeoward, S. (1988), *The Natural Rate of Unemployment?*, Buckingham: The Employment Research Centre at The University of Buckingham.

Davies, G. (1985), *Governments Can Affect Unemployment*, London: Employment Institute.

Dawson, G. (1988), *The Costs of Unemployment Versus the Costs of Inflation*, Buckingham: The Employment Research Centre at The University of Buckingham.

Department of Employment (1986), *Employment Gazette*, **94**, (6), London: HMSO, July.

Dilnot, A.W. and Morris, C.N. (undated), 'Estimating the Costs of Unemployment', Institute of Fiscal Studies Working Paper No. 27.

Dornbusch, R. and Fischer, S. (1987), *Macroeconomics*, New York: McGraw-Hill.

Feldstein, M. (1974), 'Unemployment compensation: adverse incentives and distributional anomalies', *National Tax Journal*, **27**, June, 231–44.

Fender, J. (1990), *Inflation: A Contemporary Perspective*, London and New York: Harvester Wheatsheaf.

Fischer, S. (1986), *Indexing, Inflation and Economic Policy*, Cambridge, MA: MIT Press.

Fischer, S. and Modigliani, F. (1986), 'Towards an understanding of the real effects and costs of inflation', in Fischer (1986).

Foster, J. (1976), 'The redistributive effect of inflation on building society shares and deposits 1961–74', *Bulletin of Economic Research*, **28**, 68–75.

Freeman, R. (1983), 'Crime and Unemployment', in J.Q. Wilson (ed.), *Crime and Public Policy*, San Francisco: Institute for Contemporary Studies.

Frey, B.S. and Schneider, F. (1978), 'An empirical study of politico-economic interaction in the U.S.', *Review of Economics and Statistics*, **60**, May, 174–83.

Friedman, M. (1968), 'The role of monetary policy', *American Economic Review*, **58**, 1–17.

Friedman, M. (1977), *Inflation and Unemployment: the New Dimension of Politics*, IEA Occasional Paper No. 51, London: Institute of Economic Affairs.

Friedman, M. (1991), *Monetarist Economics*, Oxford: Basil Blackwell.

Fry, V. and Pashardes, P. (1985), 'Distributional aspects of inflation: Who has suffered most?', *Fiscal Studies*, **6**, 21–9.

Geuss, R. (1981), *The Idea of Critical Theory*, Cambridge: Cambridge University Press.

Gordon, R.J. and Hall, R.E. (1980), 'Arthur M. Okun 1928–80', *Brookings Papers on Economic Activity*, **1**, 1–5.

Gowland, D.H. (1983), 'Inflation: Some New Perspectives', in D.H. Gowland (ed.), *Modern Economic Analysis 2*, London: Butterworth.

Gowland, D.H. (1990), *Understanding Macroeconomics*, Aldershot: Edward Elgar.

Gravelle, H.S.E., Hutchinson, G. and Stern, J. (1981), 'Mortality and unemployment: A critique of Brenner's time series analysis', *The Lancet* (ii), 675–9.

Greaves, J.P. and Hollingsworth, D.F. (1966), 'Trends in food consumption in the United Kingdom', *World Review of Nutrition and Dietetics*, **6**, 34–89.

Hargreaves Heap, S.P. (1980), 'Choosing the wrong "natural" rate: Accelerating inflation or decelerating employment and growth?', *Economic Journal*, **90**, 611–20.

Hayek, F. (1945), 'The use of knowledge in society', *American Economic Review*, **35**, (4), September, 519–30.

Hendry, D.F. (1980), 'Econometrics: alchemy or science?', *Economica*, **47**, 387–406.

Hibbs, D.A. (1987), *The Political Economy of Industrial Democracies*, Cambridge, MA: Harvard University Press.

Hicks, J. (1974), *The Crisis in Keynesian Economics*, Oxford: Basil Blackwell.

Higham, D. and Tomlinson, J. (1982), 'Why do governments worry about inflation?', *National Westminster Bank Quarterly Review*, May, 2–13.

Hillier, B. (1986), *Macroeconomics: Models, Debates and Developments*, Oxford: Basil Blackwell.

H.M. Treasury (1981), *Economic Progress Report*, No. 130, February.

Hughes, J.J. and Perlman, R. (1984), *The Economics of Unemployment*, Brighton: Wheatsheaf.

Hughes, P.R. and Hutchinson, G. (1986), 'Changing characteristics of male unemployment flows 1972–81', *Employment Gazette*, **94**, (8), September, 365–8.

Jahoda, M. (1982), *Employment and Unemployment: A Social-Psychological Analysis*, Cambridge: Cambridge University Press.

Junankar, P.N. (1985), *Costs of Unemployment*, Brussels: Commission of the European Communities.

Kessel, R.A. and Alchian, A.A. (1960), 'The meaning and validity of the inflation-induced lag of wages behind prices', *American Economic Review*, **50**, 43–66.

Keynes, J.M. (1931), *Essays in Persuasion*, London: Macmillan.

Knight, K.G. (1987), *Employment: An Economic Analysis*, London: Croom Helm.

Laidler, D.E.W. and Parkin, J.M. (1975), 'Inflation – a survey', *Economic Journal*, **85**, 741–809.

Layard, R. (1986), *How to Beat Unemployment*, Oxford: Oxford University Press.

Layard, R. and Nickell, S. (1985), 'The causes of British unemployment', *National Institute Economic Review*, February, 62–85.

Lindbeck, A. and Snower, D.J. (1988), 'Union Activity, Unemployment Persistence and Wage–Employment Ratchets', in Cross (1988).

Mallier, T. and Shafto, T. (1989), *Economics of Labour Markets and Management*, London: Hutchinson.

Matthews, K.G.P. (1989), 'The UK economic renaissance', *Economics*, **25**, Part 3, (107), Autumn, 103–10.

Matthews, K.G.P. and Minford, A.P.L. (1987), 'Mrs. Thatcher's economic policies 1979–87', *Economic Policy*, **5**, October, 57–101.

Meltzer, M. (1969), *Brother, Can You Spare a Dime? The Great Depression 1929–33*, New York: Alfred A. Knopf, Inc.

Metcalf, D. (1987), 'Labour Market Flexibility and Jobs: A Survey of Evidence from OECD Countries with Special Reference to Europe', in R. Layard and L. Calmfors, *The Fight Against Unemployment*, Cambridge, MA: MIT Press.

Minford, A.P.L. (1985), *Unemployment: Cause and Cure*, Oxford: Basil Blackwell.

Minford, A.P.L. and Hilliard, G.W. (1978), 'The Costs of Variable Inflation', in M. Artis and A.R. Nobay (eds.), *Contemporary Economic Analysis*, London: Croom Helm.

Minford, A.P.L. and Peel, D. (1981), 'Is the government's economic strategy on course?', *Lloyds Bank Review*, **140**.

Minford, A.P.L. and Peel, D. (1983), *Rational Expectations and the New Macroeconomics*, Oxford: Martin Robertson.

Mueller, D.C. (1989), *Public Choice II*, Cambridge: Cambridge University Press.

Newell, A. and Symons, J. (1986), 'Corporatism, *laissez-faire* and the rise in unemployment', Working Paper No. 853, Centre for Labour Economics, London School of Economics.

OECD (Organization for Economic Co-operation and Development) (1987), 'Who are the unemployed? Measurement issues and their policy implications', *OECD Employment Outlook*, Paris: OECD, September, 125–41.

OECD (1988), *OECD Employment Outlook: Historical Statistics*, Paris: OECD.

Okun, A. (1962), 'Potential GNP: its measurement and significance', *Proceedings of the Business and Economics Statistics Section of the American Statistical Association*, Washington, D.C.: ASA, 98–104; reprinted (1970) as Appendix in *Political Economy of Prosperity*, Washington, D.C.: Brookings Institution.

Opinion Research and Communication (1986), *The Unemployed and the Black Economy*, London: Opinion Research and Communication.

Phillips, A.W. (1958), 'The relationship between unemployment and the rate of change of money wage rates in the United Kingdom 1861–1957', *Economica*, **24**, 283–99.

Price, S. (1988), 'Unemployment and Worker Quality', in Cross (1988).

Proctor, N. (1987), *The UK Economy*, Wirral: Checkmate Gold.

Rowthorn, R. (1977), 'Conflict, inflation and money', *Cambridge Journal of Economics*, **1**, 215–39.

Samuelson, P.A. and Nordhaus, W.D. (1985), *Economics*, New York: McGraw-Hill.

Sargent, T.J. (1986), *Rational Expectations and Inflation*, New York: Harper & Row.

Smith, A.D., Hitchens, D.M.W.N. and Davies, S.W. (1982), *International Industrial Productivity: A Comparison of Britain, America and Germany*, Cambridge: Cambridge University Press.

Smithin, J.N. (1990), *Macroeconomics After Thatcher and Reagan*, Aldershot: Edward Elgar.

Soskice, D. (1983), 'Collective bargaining and economic policies', Manpower and Social Affairs Committee (MAS 83) **23**, Paris: OECD.

Tarling, R. (1982), 'Unemployment and crime', *Home Office Research Bulletin*, **14**.

Thirlwall, A.P. (1983), 'What are the estimates of the natural rate measuring?', *Oxford Bulletin of Economics and Statistics*, **45**.

Thomas, S. (1986), 'The costs of inflation', *Economic Review*, **4**, (2), November, 26–30.

Tobin, J. (1972), 'Inflation and unemployment', *American Economic Review*, **62**, 1–18.

Wall, N. (1990), *Money and Banking*, London and Glasgow: Collins Educational.

Warr, P. (1987), *Work, Unemployment and Mental Health*, Oxford: Oxford University Press.

Whiteside, N. (1987), 'The Social Consequences of Interwar Unemployment', in S. Glyn and A. Booth (eds), *The Road to Full Employment*, London: Allen & Unwin.

Index